What people are saying about …

CRY LIKE A MAN

"The souls of men are begging to cry and it's time to release the pain. *Cry Like a Man* is a key that Jason Wilson is using to unlock the door for men of all ethnicity to release that pain through tears, transparency, and love rather than through fighting, unresolved anger, and abuse."

—**Lewis Howes**, entrepreneur; *New York Times* bestselling author of *The School of Greatness*

"Jason Wilson is a gift to our nation that's enslaved by a dangerous and ridiculous understanding of masculinity. He's coaching us how to rear real men who know that emotions empower us, growing our capacity for courage, love, faith, hope, and so much more. As the Irish proverb says, 'Never trust a warrior who cannot cry.' He's creating a new kind of warrior. Learn from him. Support him. Join him."

—**Paul Coughlin**, founder and president of The Protectors; bestselling author of *No More Christian Nice Guy: When Being Nice—Instead of Good—Hurts Men, Women, and Children*

"I am so excited about Jason Wilson's new book, *Cry Like a Man*. Through personal stories and lessons that apply to all, Wilson shows us the power of connecting with our emotions in an increasingly disconnected world. This is a must-read for any brother seeking to better understand what he feels and why and for any sister seeking to discern the same."

—**Joshua Dubois**, CEO of Values Partnerships;
former White House faith-based advisor
to President Barack Obama; bestselling
author of *The President's Devotional*

"Jason Wilson writes a new narrative in the hearts of our black boys, one that liberates them to be the whole beautiful human beings God designed them to be."

—**Trabian Shorters**, founder and CEO of
BMe Network; coauthor of *New York Times*
bestseller *Reach: 40 Black Men Speak on
Living, Leading, and Succeeding*

"Jason Wilson is a transformational leader with a God-given ability to stand conventional wisdom on its head, unearthing the power found in struggle, pain, and compassion. Jason's life is an authentic testament to the manner, in which God uses trials, tears, and triumph to purge trauma and life's losses from the hearts of men. The truth found within this book will empower men of all ethnicities with the tools needed to break free from emotional incarceration."

—**Rodney Bullard**, Vice President of Community Affairs,
Chick-fil-A, Inc.; Executive Director, Chick-fil-A Foundation

"Growing up playing football, you are taught to never show weakness. No matter what the situation was, I was told to always 'be a man' and suck it up. Unfortunately, that mentality forced me to bottle up my emotions, causing some long-term negative effects and conflicts in my life. Jason Wilson is leading the way to freedom from emotional incarceration."

—**Reggie Bush**, Heisman Trophy
Winner; Super Bowl Champion

"Jason Wilson's incredible interactions with young boys will make you cry. Exhibiting strength in all its forms—physical, emotional, spiritual—he connects with the students at Detroit's Cave of Adullam Transformational Training Academy in a way that both empowers and inspires them to strive for their wildest dreams and to know with certainty that they are indeed attainable. In *Cry Like a Man*, Wilson shares his remarkable journey through unspeakable loss to wholeness and fulfillment. Every young man needs a Jason Wilson in his life. Through *Cry Like a Man*, many will find one."

—**Chris Broussard**, NBA analyst
and broadcaster; FOX Sports

"Jason Wilson is one of the leading voices and practitioners in the nation when it comes to providing black boys and young men with a God-inspired blueprint for growing into emotionally healthy men. I've witnessed first-hand his transformational teachings and loving leadership that happens in The Cave of Adullam, and I am so encouraged by the potential of his book to spread his empowering message to the many hearts and minds that desperately need to hear it."

—**Shawn Dove**, CEO of the Campaign
for Black Male Achievement

Cry
Like
a
Man

JASON WILSON

Cry Like a Man

FIGHTING *for* FREEDOM *from*
EMOTIONAL INCARCERATION

DAVID C COOK

transforming lives together

CRY LIKE A MAN
Published by David C Cook
4050 Lee Vance Drive
Colorado Springs, CO 80918 U.S.A.

Integrity Music Limited, a Division of David C Cook
Brighton, East Sussex BN1 2RE, England

The graphic circle C logo is a registered trademark of David C Cook.

Library of Congress Control Number 2018947997
ISBN 978-0-8307-7594-1
eISBN 978-0-8307-7676-4

The Team: Alice Crider, Kimberly Shumate,
Rachael Stevenson, Kayla Fenstermaker, Susan Murdock
Cover Design: James Hershberger
Cover Image: Greg Zonca Photography

Printed in the United States of America
First Edition 2019

9 10 11 12 13 14 15 16 17 18

021722

To every man who is tired of not being able to say he is tired.

CONTENTS

FOREWORD

I was relieved when I met Jason Wilson and heard his story and revelation. I clearly related well to his story, but I admit that I never knew I could be delivered from what he so eloquently refers to as emotional incarceration. The way I grew up I couldn't help but become callous and numb. I was a young black man searching for identity in my surroundings.

Little did I know, who I was and would become would be later found on the inside. The most defining years of my youth were spent living in South Philadelphia in a housing project called Passyunk Homes. It was low-income housing meant primarily for woman and children, but some men were allowed to live there. A few of the couples were even married. It was a very active neighborhood and criminal behavior was at a high volume. Drug dealers and their associates occupied many of the street corners. They demanded respect from everyone and was ready to render a consequence to anyone failing to demonstrate that respect.

These were the only men available to teach me about manhood. The married and responsible men were around too, but somehow, they remained out of my reach. I'd watch them leave the projects in the morning as I went to school and they went to work, and I'd notice them return later that afternoon while we were outside playing. They were always coming or going, never stopping or talking. Never correcting or advising. They just seemed to not care as they passed by. It may have been the only way they knew how to keep themselves focused and committed.

The dealers on the other hand were always around and ready to instruct me on how to "be a man," how to gain respect and provide for my loved ones. They stressed to me the importance of having money. They said the more money I had was equal to me having more power, and that power is what people respected. I was taught that crying is a form of weakness and I should avoid it at all costs. I was made to believe it was the only way I'd survive in such an unstable and hostile environment.

So, when my beloved grandfather died, I didn't cry.

When my friend Amanda was raped and murdered by her stepfather (I still remember the weight of that pain today), I didn't cry.

When my favorite cousin Buggy was shot and killed over a less than an ounce of marijuana, I refused to let the tears flow.

I thought strength was measured by how well I could hold back my tears under pressure. Even at the age of fifteen when I was shot by two guys on my way home to the projects, I didn't cry.

Eight shots, three hit me at point blank range—no tears. I turned and watched them run away and all I could think about was how angry and betrayed I felt. I hadn't done anything to deserve this; I had never shot anyone. I wasn't a dealer; I wasn't a thief, just an aspiring rap artist hoping to get money the legal way.

Tragedy after tragedy, PTSD, and a porn addiction all before the age of sixteen. I never knew how to properly process my emotions. I still don't at times. However, an encounter I had with the Most High at age twenty showed me that my identity is found not in my own strength but in His.

His Word has taught me that true manhood is seen in my ability to make mature decisions, live a disciplined life and be a servant to others, instead of possessing a careless self-serving, self-preserving mind-set. Many men today who share my past experiences feel like there's no way to cope with pain and hurt other than violence, reckless living, or passivity.

I believe Mr. Wilson's efforts to inspire, empower, and educate through his story will help many men feel our way through the trauma we've experienced so we can process and express our emotions in a healthy way.

Eshon Burgundy

Christian hip-hop artist

PROLOGUE

Men: We've scaled the heights, lifted and carried enormous burdens, sailed vast oceans, and have even broken free from the atmosphere that enfolds us from birth to death to fly among the stars. We mine the minerals and metals of the earth and create incredible machines that serve to propel us to our next aspiration. Yet amid all the risk and reward, the dilemmas and dangers, and the thrilling advances we've made, men have yet to conquer the most basic human ability—to cry.

Want to hear something shocking? It's impossible to be strong all the time.

With all the theories, credos, and misleading mantras—"Man up," "No pain, no gain," not to be outdone by the mother of all misguided intelligence, "Real men don't cry"—we have been deceived into suppressing our emotions to impress others; there's simply no room for weakness. If we're struck in our hearts, our health, or our wallets, there's no room for weakness. When we vent, we're perceived as complainers. When we hurt, we're wimps. When we're tired, we're being lazy. When we fight, we're rebels. When we're discouraged, we're depressed. When we hesitate, we're double-minded, and when

19

we cry, we're soft. With all these predetermined judgments about us, it's no wonder why so many of us "fake it to make it."

From childhood through early puberty then into manhood, we're conditioned to swallow our pain, expressing little but indifference and detachment about the chaos around us. It only makes sense that internalized stress and confusion build over time, creating a force that will eventually find a release hatch. And we all know what that looks like: self-medication, aggression, violence, until we finally hit the wall and break. And how many people do we take down with us along this destructive path of denial and pretense? Family members, girlfriends, wives, children ... ourselves.

I realized after a lifetime of holding it all in—the injuries from cruelty, neglect, and the loss of so many loved ones—that men couldn't and shouldn't have to withstand the pressure they were never designed to endure alone. The barriers I had subconsciously built, brick by agonizing brick, were merely a defense that was keeping the damage inside—pushing it down deeper and deeper. I couldn't control it. I couldn't control anything. I was a prisoner of my own emotional incarceration without the slightest idea of how I got there. The key was right in front of me; I just couldn't see it.

Suppressed feelings of anger and anxiety in men have reached epidemic levels, changing the landscape of society within families, schools, cities, and ultimately within prisons. And if it's not addressed now, it's simply going to kill us. It's my prayer that as you read this book and open your heart, you may see a little of your own journey within its pages—stories of trials and triumphs enabling you to unlock the cell you've been living in for far too long.

God (whom I often refer to as "the Most High") has played an enormous role in releasing the inner turmoil of my past. His presence wasn't something I was aware of early on, but as I grew older, losing my way in the critical decisions that would shape my future, I struggled with His very existence. Even the name "Jesus" held little importance. Paintings of Him cradling lambs or bouncing children on His knee seemed less than masculine, even "soft." I rarely thought about His stunning bravery—willingly submitting to the brutality of evil men, even being nailed to a cross—and what it actually meant.

As my relationship with the Most High developed, I began to use the Hebrew name *Yahushua* when referring to Christ, and you'll notice that name throughout this book. But many times you'll see "Yah" used for both the Father and the Son, as they are and will forever be One. It's personal and reflects the greatness of who They are to me ...

Heavenly Father, Savior, Friend.

In the time I spent getting to know Yahushua, my desire to empower other men became stronger. I asked my pastor, Gregory Alexander, to teach a men's Bible study on discipleship. To my surprise, he chose to focus on David and his mighty men instead of on Yahushua and His disciples. We started in the cave of Adullam—the place where David fled for his life. After a brief discussion, the class moved on, but I didn't. Something intrigued me about this cave.

The tangible result of my research is The Cave of Adullam Transformational Training Academy (CATTA) under the umbrella of The Yunion—a nonprofit organization I launched in Detroit in 2003. As I began to identify the direct connection between male fear and transparency, and the freedom that comes with being vulnerable, I created CATTA's Emotional Stability Training. Martial arts and biblical principles are used to teach boys and young men how to introspectively conquer their negative emotions instead of succumbing to them.

My passion and pursuit in telling my story in this book is to help boys and men find their strength to become courageously transparent about their own brokenness and to shed light on the symptoms, causes, and effects of childhood trauma and "father wounds." To free them from emotional incarceration—to see their minds renewed, souls weaned, and relationships restored.

Cry Like a Man is my own story. It has strong elements of racial terror because that has shaped my journey. Ultimately, it is the tale of how I came to overcome every source of anger, hatred, and self-condemnation that had kept me in an emotional prison.

No matter what your age, ethnicity, or social status, you can break the cycle and escape the mental prison that keeps you confined to the limits of misconstrued masculinity. Learn to feel without fear. Accept that you're not a superhero and remove the cape. As men, our "Kryptonite" is the grinding lifestyle that keeps us working when we need to rest, fighting when we need to seek peace, and worrying when we need to pray.

As you walk through the past with me in the pages ahead, my deep desire is that you will discover the power, love, and self-control it takes to truly cry like a man.

1

THE CONVICTION
OF ESTES WRIGHT

No one is born hating another person because of the color of their
skin, or his background, or his religion. People must learn to hate.
And if they can learn to hate, they can be taught to love, for love
comes more naturally to the human heart than its opposite.

Nelson Mandela, *Long Walk to Freedom*

Like red ink spilled on a black-and-white page—so black and
white—the blood of Estes Wright poured out. His face, disfigured
from the sustained and brutal beating of six white men. His fiercely
loyal heart pulled and stretched beyond its pain threshold with its
labored pounding growing weaker as the authorities stood over him,
watching. It was 1935 when Estes lay dying in the jailhouse in Fort
Pierce, Florida. A fresh cord of trauma scarring his neck squeezed

a death rattle from his throat as the life drained from my grandfather ... *and no one did a thing to stop it.*

Estes Wright had the kind of charisma that was hard to miss—a blessing or a curse depending on the company. A fruit picker by trade, Estes, unlike his peers, had a dynamic personality and strong sense of self that left a lasting impression on everyone he met. But on no one more than his young, impressionable brother-in-law, James.

Estes and his wife, Margaret, were in their midthirties and expecting their sixth child. They had grown up in caring, churchgoing families that kept them loved and protected, if only within the safety of their homes. The couple were radical Christians, though Margaret was more religious and Estes less conforming. Her passionate relationship with Christ went well beyond weekly Sunday school and the annual homecoming potlucks. It was her devotion to God that reinforced her husband's identity in the One who created him—the One who created everyone in His own image and equally loved them. An image with no dominating color, only brilliant hues of humanity.

Estes believed in the dignity and integrity of every individual, no matter how light or dark his or her skin—a dangerous ideal for a Negro in the pre–World War II Deep South.

There was no questioning that Estes was fearless, at times unapologetically. It was this strength and determination that a man of color could regret. But Estes couldn't be anything less than what God made him to be. He wasn't the type of person to drop his chin and talk to the floor when a white man asked him a question or to do what he was told simply by virtue of his race. No, that would never do for a man like Estes Wright. And while his peers admired him for having the courage that disregarded both prevailing racial lines and the tension that came with looking a white man in the eye, his conviction would be tested.

It was common knowledge Estes carried a gun; it was less common for a black man to bear arms in those days. He was confident, clever, and filled with a dignity that got him noticed—on both sides of town but for two very different reasons. I think that's probably why he kept that revolver tucked away but always close at hand. To condone Colored condemnation and white superiority went against every fiber woven into Estes's soul. But skin color and social stature had little to do with the way Estes treated others. The fact was, he treated everyone with the respect—or contempt—that person showed him.

My grandfather's indomitable spirit was never more noticed than during the Great Depression when the United States government began to distribute surplus food to the starving masses. People were suffering regardless of their color, gender, age, or religion. Suddenly the great divide was shrinking as the basic necessities of life disappeared, leaving black and white equally deprived. From coast to coast, long lines formed outside soup kitchens, bringing all walks of life together—closer than many preferred.

Two lines—"Whites Only" and "Coloreds Only."

During these turbulent times, Negroes waited obediently for the white townsfolk to fill their gunnysacks with food before they were allowed to enter the building to pick through the scraps left behind. But deep in the pit of his stomach, Estes knew no one had the right to tell him to "mind his place." There was only one place for him, and that was beneath the almighty hand that bore the nail scars for all humankind. To wait in a segregated line was more than offensive to Estes. It was an abomination. To Estes, pain and poverty held the same unbearable degradation for all.

Estes wouldn't stand it. Maybe it was the press of the crowd or the sweltering heat of the Florida sun, but I suspect it was the shame seared into each face of color bending beneath the weight of daily humiliation. He felt and saw their desperation—shoulders bowed, nerves frayed, and spirits broken—and it pushed Estes into brave defiance as, time after time, he strode past the queue of blacks, then the whites, and finally past the sheriff standing next to the provisions.

Estes, with his brother-in-law James, boldly filled their bags with all the food they needed, without resistance. The sheriff remembered the gun within Estes's pocket. Then the two would walk out with groceries in tow to the disgust and anger of the fairer citizens still waiting in line. James learned much from Estes's courage—lessons depicted in the acclaimed book, *The Golden Thirteen*. It wasn't long after that when the indelible courage of Estes Wright would challenge the status quo once more.

Whether by established law or small-town edict, it was a crime in Fort Pierce for a Colored to fish off the town's bridge after dark, one of the many restrictions placed on the black community in that troubling time. But in true Estes fashion, he believed he had every right to fish from that bridge or any other whenever he pleased. And armed with his revolver and with James by his side, he went down to the bridge one night. An hour hadn't passed before three white men appeared.

"What the [expletive] are you niggers doing down here fishing at night?" one spouted.

"Because we want to," Estes answered as he pulled out his .38. "I'll give you ten seconds to get off this bridge. If I ever see you again …" Estes took aim at the man's head.

That was enough to send the men running, knowing Estes was never one to bluff.

I've sometimes wondered what I would have done had I been there—hearing those racial slurs, receiving that kind of hate, fighting the social order in a highly charged and dangerous America. Would I have reacted the same way as my grandfather? Was his defense worth it? Was this one tiny moment of prejudice, in a lifetime of equally oppressive moments, worth Estes's strong response? Would the repercussions of that small victory on the bridge and his fight against bigotry and intolerance make a meaningful contribution to the push and pull that finally arrived in the form of civil rights thirty years later?

Yes, of course. Freedom will always want to fly. Peace will wrap its arms around fear until it is smothered. Love will always outshine hate until only the brilliant light of truth remains. And a man's life will always find its purpose in battle, just as Estes found his.

As another day dawned much like any other, Estes grabbed a ride from a friend, and together they drove through streets of familiar faces and friendly waves. Soon the blocks changed as the hospitable smiles gave way to the predominantly white center of town. As they slowed and stopped at a traffic light, six white men suddenly converged on the car.

They pulled Estes out of the vehicle and dragged him away as onlookers did nothing. I figure those watching must have felt one of two things: either they were too frightened to help him, or they wondered what took the town's white men so long to rein in the "uppity nigger" too high and mighty for his own good. The men beat him so savagely that the bones in his face and head shattered. They attacked him until the blood disguised him; his swollen eye sockets and torn flesh took away his identity. Generations of hate came to bear on Estes until he was unrecognizable.

But everyone knew it was Estes Wright—a man humiliated, beaten, and about to be hung on a tree. On a day that started out like any other day, six men viciously strung up my grandfather with a rope and lynched him in broad daylight in Fort Pierce, Florida, in the United States—the world's greatest beacon of freedom and democracy.

He was a black man who lived life as if he had every privilege of a white man, and *that* was unforgivable. He was secure in his own skin yet unprotected. He was strong in who he was yet never enough. He was confident in his color yet still subject to the offense it caused. He had every attribute any man could hope for yet was still inadequate to withstand the racism that ruled the era.

Estes Wright hung by the neck, but they hadn't killed him. Not yet.

The news of the violence quickly spread through town, and James and his sister Carrie reached the jailhouse along with several hundred people after Estes's limp body had been carried into the building. By the time they had dropped him on a hard wooden bench, his life was leaving him. James and Carrie entered to find him there, grotesque, unconscious, and slipping away. Carrie tried to wipe the blood from his face, and James noticed how his head was as "soft as cotton" from the relentless beating. They were both thrown out by the sheriff to leave Estes to pass from this life without family, friends, or pastor present. Just surrounded by men who hated his very existence.

I still think about the authorities bringing him back to the jail. Not the hospital. Not the morgue.

The jail.

Estes wasn't a threat. He wasn't a criminal. He was just a man— one who knew his own worth and had the righteous audacity to forego the color lines and the back of the bus and brave the town bridge after dark. He was a human being struck down simply by virtue of his pigment and lineage. I go over it in my mind, and as I reflect on everything they did to him in his last hours on earth, I keep coming up with the same question: *What made them cut him down?*

I wish it was pity, but history tells me that's a false hope. Dead black bodies hanging from Southern trees was not an uncommon sight in the Jim Crow South. Even the songstress Billie Holiday solemnly sang about it in her 1939 recording titled "Strange Fruit."

Black bodies swinging in the southern breeze
Strange fruit hanging from the poplar trees[1]

These evil men may have been finished with my grandfather, but the struggle wasn't over. It had only changed into something else. It became obvious that law enforcement and the murderers were cut from the same cloth, and my grandfather's family was harassed night after night by the police. They pounded on their door to intimidate them in case Estes had planted his ideals in the minds of his relatives. Even private citizens of Fort Pierce—racist whites— would kidnap Estes's brother-in-law Sam in the middle of the night for joyrides. They threatened him, threw him into multiple cars to lengthen the ordeal, and on some occasions locked him in a jail cell for "safekeeping."

Months of aggression finally took their toll on Sam. He was taken to South Carolina to recover from a nervous breakdown. The family's neighbors stopped speaking to them, anxious that they would soon become the next target. The aftermath of Estes's murder created panic throughout the black community, resulting in the alienation of Estes's family. My family. Everyone was terrified, and the stress of simply living became an enormous burden.[2]

Neither the police nor the murder suspects were ever charged with a crime.

The only conviction was that of my grandfather Estes Wright.

NOTES

1. Billie Holiday, vocalist, "Strange Fruit," by Abel Meeropol, recorded April 20, 1939, single on Commodore Classics in Swing, Commodore Records, 78 rpm.
2. James E. Hair, "Son of a Slave," in *The Golden Thirteen: Recollections of the First Black Naval Officers*, ed. Paul Stillwell (Annapolis, MD: Bluejacket Books, 1993), chap. 10.

2

THE NEMESIS

Emotions are great servants but poor masters.

Kajana Cetshwayo

It was 1967 when the riots broke out—one of the bloodiest race wars in twentieth-century America, also known as the "long, hot summer." The Detroit riot started at 4:00 a.m. on July 23 when police raided an illegal gin joint. It grew into five days of looting, arson, assault, and murder.

After all was said and done—after the governor sent thousands of National Guard troops and President Lyndon Johnson called in the Eighty-Second Airborne—the death toll had reached forty-three with injuries topping 1,180. Among the 7,231 arrested, half of them didn't have a criminal history—the youngest was four years old and the oldest was eighty-two. More than 2,500 businesses were looted or burned along with apartment buildings, leaving 388 families homeless.[1]

Detroit was in shambles—a toxic, racially charged city—when my mother moved there in December of 1967.

But let's rewind. It was in 1953 when my mother, Etta Marie, married a man named Sinclair Sr., a raging alcoholic who beat her when he needed an excuse to vent, which was often. There in Fort Lauderdale, Florida, she gave birth to two of my brothers, Sinclair Jr. and Larry. They were her emotional refuge until they also became the targets of their father's impulsive anger. Though his physical abuse would come and go—usually with the contents of the bottle in his hand—the mental wounds he inflicted sank deeper than his fists could ever hope to reach.

For nine long years they endured his random cruelty. My brother Sinclair once told me that at dinner one evening, his father slapped him with the flat side of a butcher knife just because he accidentally spilled food on his pajamas. In another instance, he was so blind drunk and furious that he grabbed his shotgun and fired it into the floor, the gaping hole a reflection of a crumbling family foundation where fear hung in the air like gunpowder.

As I grew up listening to the horror stories about Sinclair Sr.— his reckless exploits and all the pain he caused—I started to hate him. He was the villain who always won. And though I may have wanted to beat him into a mentally impaired state, Sinclair wanted to flat-out kill him. And if God's grace hadn't intervened, he would have fulfilled that dream.

As I got a little older, I could scarcely make sense of how a man could be so hateful toward his own wife and children. My mother was a beautiful, talented woman, and my brothers inherited her good looks and giftedness. Sinclair Sr. had the kind of family other men envied—everything that could have brought him unspeakable joy. But it wasn't to be. My mother had already endured the childhood trauma of her father's murder and being ostracized by her community. She deserved a man who cherished her and respected that kind of strength.

What was it in Sinclair Sr.'s past that could have created so much misery for him in the present? There had to be a reason.

There's always a reason.

I'm told that at the end of those nine tumultuous years of marriage, my mother gathered the courage to leave with my brothers and file for divorce. Not a popular course of action in the early 1960s, especially for a young woman with children. But the thought of her kids living in the line of fire—literally—was no longer bearable. After the marriage ended, she met my father, Oliver Wilson Jr., through her brother, Clarence Wright.

Finding a man who loved her and was also willing to take in her two boys was a godsend. They were married in 1967 and moved to Detroit in December of that year, but they left my brothers in Florida with their aunt while they settled in. It must have seemed like a miracle—a solid male figure bringing security and stability after such a detrimental relationship. But not everybody was happy with the union. Sinclair Jr. for one. He wasn't thrilled with Mama for going back into the lion's den or for moving to Detroit.

For a year, the boys waited.

It was January of 1968 when Mama sent for my brothers. At fourteen and twelve years old, they traded the humid eighty-five-degree weather of Fort Lauderdale for Michigan's bone-chilling eight below. It was the first time they had ever experienced snow, and their hands and feet had never been so cold. Along with a new house and neighborhood and the unfamiliar racial tension, they were now surrounded by junior high students who openly smoked cigarettes and blatantly lived "the thug life." Clearly out of their element, Sinclair and Larry had abruptly landed in Detroit's inner city with its unfamiliar rules and confrontational lifestyle.

Bigotry was new to them, or maybe they had just been too young to recognize it before. But they did now.

As the weeks and months melted together, Sinclair and Larry began to develop friendships as well as form new opinions. Detroit was unlike any place they had ever seen, with black people living successful lives. Fathers who were doctors, lawyers, and executives working for Motown. High-ranking employees at the big three: General Motors, Ford, and Chrysler. They wore expensive clothes and drove luxury cars.

But Detroit had another side—a darker, seedier side. Its streets were deceptively deadly, and one careless decision could cost you your life.

Larry was a social butterfly who got along with everyone. Bestowed with the gift of gab, he easily made friends, male and female. He was also cunning and impressionable and not entirely particular about whom he invited into his circle. In hindsight, maybe that was his only mistake.

Sinclair, on the other hand, was serious and focused, and he steered clear of foolishness. He could also be sullen and reclusive, which resulted in him spending long solitary hours with few friends. I suppose my mother gave him the space, believing every family had at least one moody teenager within its ranks.

Our mom continued to heal from her first marriage, though she now suffered from anxiety due to years of abuse. Oliver remained stern and began to show signs of stress with growing impatience and increasing absence. I realize every blended household has its share of dysfunction, but ours had an underlying friction—a resistance within—where each piece of the domestic puzzle didn't quite fit. It may not have been clear from the outside, but pressure was building.

In the winter of 1969, the news of my mother's unexpected pregnancy was a welcome mental break from the daily drama. The promise of something precious gave her renewed purpose. My father, however, was far less enthusiastic. Oliver didn't share the excitement about the coming birth. In fact, he was livid. With three daughters from a previous marriage, he didn't want or need another child, especially in his forties.

His contempt for the unplanned addition lasted throughout the entire nine months, and during that time he repeatedly reminded my mother that he would *not* be at the hospital during labor or the birth.

Turns out, he was bluffing.

Unbeknownst to many, my dad wanted a son more than he ever let on. But with 1970s ultrasound machines being what they were, there wasn't any guarantee what the gender of a child would be. To brace himself for the worst, he rejected any involvement, thus tainting what should have been a truly special season in his life. His wife's growing belly was viewed as an antagonist with more power than any tiny being should be allowed. The power to either fortify his masculinity or threaten it.

After he had paced for hours across the hospital waiting room, nervously cutting a path through his poorly hidden excitement, the doctor eventually emerged from the delivery room with the news that he would be taking home a healthy baby boy. Suddenly the dark clouds hanging over his bitter angst lifted, and all was forgiven.

I was born in Detroit on August 21, 1970. Years later, his friends would tell me that my father's dearest dream came true on that day.

Now Oliver had a little boy. But little boys one day wake up as young men just as my older brothers did. Clashing titans. Sinclair's intellect served him well, and he graduated from the renowned Cass Tech High School. Holding down a job at the neighborhood drugstore, he also applied himself at the local community college during his first year of higher education. It was a common conclusion that Sinclair would end up conquering any boardroom or starting his own business. But it was his love of animals that drew him toward veterinary medicine. You could see it in everything he did—he would find success one day.

As Sinclair deliberately forged ahead, the house pulsated with the music streaming from Larry's room. It seemed that every instrument he picked up, he could play. One in particular became an extension of his hands, his personality, his passion. The guitar was by far his favorite, and the harmonious conversations he and that instrument spoke were in a language all their own. Sinclair may have excelled in academia, but Larry was fluent in melody. Sitting at his feet while he and his friends rehearsed in the basement, I would strum along on an old acoustic. He was so tall. So tall and full of life. My personal superhero who spent time with me, encouraged me, loved me.

And it was easy to love him back.

If only Sinclair and Larry could have found allies in each other, peace might have prevailed. But the two collided and made no apologies for it. Their ongoing disputes and bickering were a constant source of anguish for my mom and an endless irritant to my dad. When Sinclair finally moved to Florida to attend Indian River College his second year of school, he and Larry rarely spoke. Mama was crushed. The emotional battery she had hoped to leave behind with her first marriage had followed her, if only in an altered state.

For me, Sinclair's departure left a void in our house like a cold draft from an open door. And with my dad's presence being missed for longer periods at a time—beyond work—my mother dedicated herself to taking care of me.

But for Larry, his territory had suddenly expanded. He could stretch out and breathe without being compared to his older brother. Though he was still at home and had two more years of high school to complete, he was free to explore his own uncharted path in the world. Fearless and a natural-born leader, Larry still wasn't immune to peer pressure. And like so many black boys today, he was impressed by young men who dressed cool, drove pricey cars, got the cutest girls, and flashed the most cash.

A young man will always dream—of heroes, girls, gangstas, and extremes.

NOTE

1. Ben Cosgrove, "Detroit Burning: Photos from the 12th Street Riot, 1967," *Time*, July 22, 2012, http://time.com/3638378/detroit-burning-photos-from -the-12th-street-riot-1967/; Wendell Anthony, "Don't Be Afraid to Reflect on the Unrest of 1967," *Detroit Free Press*, May 4, 2017, www.freep.com/story /opinion/contributors/2017/05/04/detroit-riot-1967-anniversary/101292236/; Sidney Fine, "Rioters and Judges: The Response of the Criminal Justice System to the Detroit Riot of 1967," *Wayne Law Review* 33, no. 5 (1987): 1723.

3

TRAGEDY AND TEARS

You, me, or nobody is gonna hit as hard as life. But it ain't about how hard you hit. It's about how hard you can get hit and keep moving forward.

Sylvester Stallone, *Rocky Balboa*

It's expected for a young man to test the boundaries, push the envelope, and see how thin the air is outside the pocket. His testosterone is pumping, girls are flirting, and he feels invincible … that is, until he eventually meets his match.

Until that day arrived, my mother tried to push Larry back inside the lines, but it just wasn't working. Ignoring his curfew on a regular basis, he sometimes found our front doorstep only after daybreak. My father's patience ran out on the night Larry drifted into the house, smelling of marijuana, and disrespected Mama. Oliver couldn't hold it in any longer and threw a punch. I don't think my brother saw it coming, but I'm sure he felt it.

Larry could set off Oliver with one look. This rebellious teenager, like a typical young man, was easily deceived by deadly untamed emotions. In a last desperate attempt to rein him in, my parents sent him away for his junior year to live with our aunt, Louise, in Pensacola, Florida. Pushed out, quarantined, exiled ... all those thoughts must have run through his mind before leaving his friends and family.

It was plain to Larry and my dad that any regard they once shared was now gone. They had both stepped over that invisible line, from tolerance to contempt. Larry's disrespect was grounded in Oliver's womanizing, and Oliver's unwillingness to deal with his own shortcomings was not an issue up for discussion. His blatant philandering coupled with my mother's worrying was enough to put Larry on that plane, and he left.

While he was in Florida with Aunt Louise, Larry's memories of his biological dad, Sinclair Sr., flooded in with the early tide. Funny how we recall only the things that support what we want to be true. Larry wondered whether his dad was as callous as he remembered; perhaps he had changed over the years. There was only one way to know for sure.

Believing everyone deserved a second chance, Larry picked up the phone, hoping to find a man eager to reconcile and start over, a father ready to renew their relationship. With luck, Larry would hear the words he was aching for: "Come home."

Oh, the power of selective memory ... yearning for the man who slapped his older brother with a butcher knife and beat his mother senseless. Though we try to resist, the circle of life keeps twirling around an irresistible center of gravity. The core of our personal universe, the beginning of our creation—our fathers. And after vacancy has dusted off the cobwebs of our unsettled recollections, we reach out one more time.

Larry could only hope that his heart's tug would be met with a fatherly hug.

The phone rang; Sinclair Sr. picked up, and … he was still the same. The same mean, selfish person he'd always been. Larry's plea for compromise was met with the same cold resistance and unconditional rejection. The final knife dug straight into the childhood wound he had inflicted years before. There was no real reason for him to act any differently. Sinclair never paid a dime of child support, never sent the boys a birthday card or took them somewhere on vacation. No special treats like basketball tickets or a new toy just because. If there was ever a doubt (or hope) in Larry's mind about his father's true feelings, it became clear in that phone call.

A father's affirmation is foundational to a son's confidence. In retrospect, after years of helping boys heal emotionally, I can now see it was neglect and abuse that fueled my brother's misguided quest for affirmation. Redemption has been known to take a lifetime but also can be as quick as a single smile.

At the end of Larry's school year, he returned to Detroit wiser. The sunshine, scenery, and closure had washed him with an affirming sense of optimism. Everyone noticed it, and everyone was hopeful. It was so good to have him home.

As his senior year at Central High began, Larry surpassed all expectations. With his good looks and untamable personality, he single-handedly organized his school's first marching band, then became its drum major. Extraordinary ... that's what Florida A&M University (FAMU) decided when they gave him a full-ride scholarship as a music major. For the first time in so very long, Mama's pride in her wayward son was justified. Larry had done a complete 180 as he applied his talents and made genuine strides toward a successful future.

Mama had an unusual look about her that year. Finally, she was content.

———— • ————

Like any metropolitan city, Detroit had its mix of affluent neighborhoods with tree-lined streets and manicured lawns as well as urban patches of concrete and crime. Each area came with its own unique demographic. Our family was far from poor and lived in a nice middle-class neighborhood. Both of my parents were blessed with dependable jobs. Mama was an optical technician, and my father, passionately referred to by his clients as "Big O," worked as a successful barber with an impressive clientele. This meant that my brothers and I, unlike other boys growing up in that neighborhood, never needed to sell drugs for survival. We were fortunate to have the encouragement of peers and role models who promoted accountability and offered support.

Reconnecting with a close friend like "Mane," Larry regained a big brother to help him through the challenges that continued to hover around him. Mane had a couple of years on Larry and the maturity to keep his head up and his nose clean. When he graduated

Central High two years before Larry, it was no coincidence that my brother's decision-making slowly but undeniably digressed.

And despite Larry's questionable company and choices, Mane loved him. His time with Larry gradually thinned to occasionally seeing each other on the block. Still, their forged brotherhood remained strong.

Sometimes I think people feel the desire or need to recover something wrong in order to make it right. To retrieve that detestable thing that's too heartbreaking to leave the way it is. To salvage what we can before it disintegrates.

Larry returned to his familiar ways. He found a new crew—or perhaps they found him—and their influence was unmistakable. Though Larry's kind spirit and sheer likability was a blessing to many who knew him, it could also be a curse.

I think ultimately that was the reason my brother was approached by members of his own circle. Larry's charisma was perfect for drug distribution. With that infectious smile and legions of friends, he was trusted and celebrated. He had everything they needed to dominate the marketplace. And in their midst, Larry left the safety and support of his own and crossed the line into a threatening environment of unbendable loyalty and persuasive obligation—an atmosphere that didn't permit the luxury of saying no.

Larry's insolent ways toward my parents resumed and accelerated as he pushed the boundaries and tested the waters. Finally caught stealing money from Oliver, Larry would have been kicked out of the house had it not been for the FAMU scholarship. If he could only make it to the end of the school year.

The equilibrium of our home leveled off as Larry prepared to graduate. I'm sure it was a day Mama didn't think he would live long enough to see, but there he was standing on that stage in his cap and gown. He proved his mettle. He had accomplished what he set out to do. Soon the summer would be over, and he'd be on his way to Florida A&M. There was a collective sigh of relief from our family that day. Though I was only a little fella at the time, I hailed my superhero and marveled at Larry's seemingly unlimited talent. He was unstoppable. I was absolutely sure he could do anything.

——— • ———

It was late afternoon on Sunday, July 3, 1973, when Larry drove our mother's car down a neighboring block. There was still plenty of sunlight, though it was sinking steadily toward the horizon.

With a caravan trailing him, Larry's party on rims echoed the bass lines of multiple stereos bouncing on ten. Mane was on his front porch when Larry pulled over and called out to him.

"Mane, take my mother's car and park it out front of my house for me."

Mane hesitated. But with his friend leaving for FAMU soon, he would have few opportunities to show his friendship to Larry before he headed to Florida.

"All right … all right … give me the keys!" he replied, though later he would tell me it didn't feel right.

There was music blasting and girls laughing as the keys flew into Mane's outstretched hand. Still, in all the commotion, Mane noticed something strange. A group of men in a nearby white Cadillac

Fleetwood got out of their ride simultaneously and ushered Larry into their vehicle—the same car that neighbors told my mother would pick up Larry while she was at work.

The caravan sped off and out of sight.

During the exchange with Mane, my brother never let on that anything was wrong, but something wasn't right. He had left his wallet and identification under the front seat of Mama's car. It wasn't like Larry to make such a careless mistake. Careless or cautious?

Mane delivered my mother's car to our house and left.

The next morning on Monday, July 4, Larry wasn't in his bed.

A mother's intuition can prove to be unnerving and discerning. Mama tried to stay calm, but in her growing restlessness, she began calling around. No one had seen him. No one had heard from him. He had vanished.

On a day when crowds celebrated with barbecues and fireworks, our block was eerily quiet. No ribs cookin' or rockets poppin'. Only blank stares of friends and neighbors fearing the worst for my brother's safety. Mama fought her intuition until Wednesday ... the day when a certain beloved superhero finally met his match.

Larry's body was discovered by a couple of fishermen in the Belle Isle shallows. He was still wearing his superhero cape—his clothes— but the Kryptonite had done its damage.

The scream of a mother whose child has been murdered and thrown away like trash is enough to turn your blood cold. There's nothing you can compare it to. It begins in a place so deep it's difficult to reach, until it surges beyond physical, mental, and emotional limits. Your heart explodes into a million pieces, and it feels as if the soul dies with it.

Torrential tears raining down, not a sunny day in sight.

My mother lay in the arms of her best friend, Byrda, while my father made his way to the city morgue with the horrific task of identifying Larry. Despite all the disputes and scrimmages they had, my dad was truly tormented by what he saw, what he found out, and what he *didn't* find out. The description of Larry's death was vague at best. Even my father's appeals to the police for the smallest details were casually dismissed. They acted as if Larry was simply a thug—with or without a grieving mother, a little brother. No talents, no opportunities, no free ride to college. Just "another dead nigger." Just a statistic that washed up on the murky banks of the Detroit River two days before.

Sinclair was in Florida when a long-distance call came with the grim news. Initially he was in shock and refused to believe that something so horrid was true. But once he saw our grandmother Margaret weeping inconsolably, he knew Larry was gone. Then came the inescapable regrets: *What did I say to him? What* didn't *I say to him? If I could go back, what would I tell him?* My brothers didn't always get along, but they still loved each other.

The autopsy revealed that no water had entered Larry's lungs, which meant he was dead before going into the river. Larry was an expert swimmer on the high school swim team, so the thought of him drowning was absurd. Rumors abounded that he was thrown from the Belle Isle Bridge, while his girlfriend would later say that he owed money to the guys in the Caddy.

The most consistent theory of those who knew him best was that the men in the Cadillac turned a profit by using his charisma and street respect, and when Larry wanted to get out, they showed him the exit. But it was all speculation. Truth is, he was playing a game that couldn't be won.

I don't know how or why my brother was killed; I only know I miss him.

His obituary consisted of ninety words and a poem. Only ninety words to sum up his seventeen years of life, a young man who just the month before wore a graduate's smile and held a golden ticket to college. It was small type, a narrow newspaper column, a nightmare in black ink that couldn't be washed away—not with soap, tears, or the water of the Belle Isle shallows.

My mom was slowly losing her mind, initially ripping up the life-insurance check that was issued for the death of my brother. After days of consoling her, my dad eventually calmed her to the point where she could cope with the insurance company issuing a new check. Whether she had destroyed the check out of her helpless anger or survivor's guilt now that he was gone, my mother knew that no amount of money could compensate for Larry's empty bed.

First her father, now her son. Was anyone safe? And what about her youngest child? From the time Larry was killed, Mama wanted—no, she *needed*—me near her. I was a form of the Most High's grace to her.

The funeral overflowed with more than a thousand people. In attendance were Larry's closest friends, kids from school, his marching band, everyone from our neighborhood, family from out of town—even Sinclair Sr.

Larry's biological father had a right to be there, and only he knew the demons he battled when getting the news of his son's murder. He did not, however, get a warm welcome from my mother, brother, or father when he approached the limo to join us.

My dad irrefutably dog-checked him at the car door, saying, "I will [expletive] you up if you step one foot into this limo."

You could always count on my dad to let you know exactly where you stood with him. He rarely held his tongue when it came to speaking his mind, especially in the presence of someone as spineless as Sinclair Sr. It was the first time I ever saw him—the villain who always won. Or did he?

As a grown man today, I'm disturbed not only that he abandoned Larry after scarring his childhood with memories of abuse but also that he never offered one dime to help with the funeral costs. My father paid for it all, in so many ways.

I was three years old at the time, without an adult's perspective or ability to understand the gravity of what had happened. I was left to sift the wreckage through a toddler's mind. To wander into Larry's room looking for him and never finding him. To cry every night when he didn't come home. I couldn't grasp why my larger-than-life brother— my superhero—had flown away and left me without saying good-bye.

Every time the doorbell rang, I expected him to be standing there, but he never was. And he never would be again.

How I wanted just one more hug, one more laugh, one more song.

4

A HOUSE IS
NOT A HOME

*No man should tout he's the head of his house, when
he is rarely there to help make it a home.*

Zaddiyq AriYah

Our house felt different ... emptier. My brother Larry was gone,
swallowed up by the stealthy but lethal undercurrents of Detroit,
notorious for rushing young men to their deaths. Without the facts
of his murder, closure was impossible. The sun still rose in the morning and set at night, but the abrupt end to his life kept the porch
light perpetually burning. It never really goes out, even when your
last bit of emotional energy is spent.

And just as the dusk steals the light of day, my mother was mentally disappearing in front of us.

She was falling, spiraling down. Diagnosed with acute anxiety and clinical depression, Mama was barely able to function. Her nerves had turned to dust that she buried with her son, and she had changed. If it weren't for Glynda, the caring fifteen-year-old girl down the street who took care of us, I can't say what would have happened. The daughter my mother always yearned for, Glynda came to live with us for six months. She would massage my mom's back, bathe her, and cook for our family.

Then Mama started to drink and fixate on moving out of our home. After the death of her father and the harassment of the Fort Pierce police, her family had been forced to relocate. In my mother's mind, surely that was the natural progression after a homicide in the family. You move.

Thank God for my brother Sinclair.

It's true he had a rough start with his earliest lessons in fear taught by the heavy hand of his father, Sinclair Sr. A man who located the bottom of a bottle as regularly as his temper, exploding at his wife and kids. Not exactly the solid, even temperament a child needs. His dad's unpredictable and often violent nature created despair in my brother that later would be diagnosed as severe depression.

Throughout their young lives, boys are taught to withstand the strain of holding in their tears, suppressing them until it hurts. Eventually they grow into men who fear appearing vulnerable, a fate no self-respecting man can live with.

The majority of fathers I've worked with over the years truly want the best for their sons. However, because of unresolved anger associated with how they were mistreated by their own dads, they are hindered from expressing the love they longed for. As men, we have to cease fathering from our wounds and seek healing from the trauma we've received so our sons can be loved comprehensively.

———— • ————

After my mother left his father, like most sons of single mothers, my brother Sinclair became increasingly possessive of our mother. When she started dating again and considered remarrying, the anger and fear in him multiplied. It was a cycle that the 1970s medical field was ill-equipped to treat.

And as every boy growing up has a pastime—school sports, playing an instrument, shooting hoops with neighborhood kids—my brother's standard practice was sitting in a psychologist's office for weekly therapy sessions. Throughout his teens, Sinclair depended on the guidance of a mental professional in order to survive his daily bouts with depression.

In September 1974 Sinclair left for Tuskegee University to start his third year of college. While in Alabama, he met a man who showed up unexpectedly, turning out to be the closest friend he would ever know—the ultimate replacement for the unstable love of any human. I'm not sure whether Sinclair had been formally introduced to Him before that, but he knew Him now.

Yahushua—better known as Jesus—was a radical leader and the righteous, compassionate, self-sacrificing Son of the Most High God. So committed to His mission on earth, He agreed to "take the bullet" for humankind in order for Sinclair to escape his own slavery of mind and heart.

Such a companion and friend comes only once in a lifetime, and several radical Christians on campus understood the importance of giving up their human agendas for Yah's perfect plan. The emptiness that isolated Sinclair and kept him fearful for so long—all the dark and lonely corners of his psyche—was suddenly filled with light. A light so consuming that power flooded in along with a sizable group of like-minded friends.

Their Bible studies, prayer alliances, church time, and worship services centered around their dearest Confidant—the Creator and Ruler of the universe. The One who laid down His life for Sinclair more than two thousand years ago. Their bond was immediate, with a strength that only blood spilled on your behalf can provide.

When Sinclair finished the year at Tuskegee, he brought his new best Friend home with him. The Holy and radical Spirit saturated everything he did. He countered the norm, living the example of what a true man of the Most High should be. Instead of zodiac signs and naked women on his walls, he found refuge in church and his new friends there. During an era of P-Funk and soul music, Sinclair blasted Andraé Crouch in his room instead of the Funkadelic. My mother would yell for him to "Turn down that Jesus music!"

I jokingly asked her, "Mom, what's wrong with playing God's music loud?" She laughed, unable to give me a good reason.

There was one name scrawled in stars across the ceiling of Sinclair's room—the same stars shining brightly so many nights as I lay on his bed staring up at them. A name like no other.

Jesus!

With awakening knowledge of good and evil, darkness and light, demons and angels, Sinclair saw similarities between Larry and me and made it an early priority to guide me away from the land mines that sabotaged our brother.

Yah's strength and guidance saturated everything Sinclair did. He oozed faith and made an indelible mark on me as his relationship continued to flourish and grow in the shadow of the Almighty. The best way to describe it was supernatural. Putting it simply, my brother had a hotline to heaven. When he dropped a contact lens on the bathroom floor, instead of crawling on hands and knees, anxious to find it, he just closed his eyes, prayed for a minute, then looked down and it would be there. Nothing was his battle. Any struggle, no matter the size, belonged to his Friend. Sinclair knew the power of Yahushua.

Through my young eyes so willing to believe with a childlike faith, I recognized the undeniable workings of the Most High in Sinclair. It was during these impressionable years that seeds were planted in me that would later grow to equip me for my spiritual destiny. Sinclair is the main reason I am who I am today—radically righteous and sold out for Yah.

———— • ————

Mama's chronic mental health challenges tossed us from side to side as minor swells in her daily routine threatened to capsize our family's delicate keel. What she was unable to take on, the rest of us absorbed. As my dad watched his wife slowly crumble before him, he accepted that his family needed saving. He moved us into a beautiful brick ranch house on the west side of Detroit. The change of scenery was therapeutic, and my mother's depression eased. Still, she never completely recovered from Larry's death, and her attitude toward life in general was never the same. It seemed from that point on, the pain of her past had wrought a silent devastation she couldn't escape.

My father found his own way of escape—in another woman.

Word on the street was that the infidelity was linked to the mother of my half brother, Keith. Three years after Larry's death, my mom divorced my dad in 1976. They sat me down one night to tell me he was moving out, and I cried and questioned why he was leaving. His answer—that escapes me now—wasn't sufficient to soothe the crushing emotions that came with knowing my father would no longer live with us.

Had I known then that my life—through the tangled weeds and overgrowth of disappointment—would eventually be pared and pruned into a garden of blessings, maybe it wouldn't have mattered so much. But boys instinctively look to their makers—their fathers—for answers. And when there are none to be found, they fill the void with what's available. If only we could set our sights a little higher, we could see that our Maker is with us from our first step to our last breath.

———— • ————

My mother and I were close, but the shatterproof walls around her made it difficult at times for her to express love. With my father's abrupt exit came Mama's unfamiliar role of disciplinarian. By that time, I couldn't explain the hostility in me, much less stop it—anger directed straight at her.

After the divorce, my father unknowingly redefined my identity: from beloved son to burdensome boy. Our one weekly court-appointed day together saddled him with an inconvenient task rather than treasured bonding time. On the afternoons his car sat idling in front of my school, he was rarely alone. A much younger female usually sat beside him. Revolving replacements for my mother … and me. My dad's promiscuous ways began a subliminal education and taught me that being faithful to one woman was a sign of weakness and debatable masculinity.

How many women does it take to please one man? I wondered.

As a convenient defense for his impatience, I was blamed for things that, as my father, Oliver should have taken the time to teach me. It's unnerving how the littlest things in my past never leave, never diminish over time.

For example, I loved seafood. On one of our weekly visits, my father took me to a popular lobster restaurant for what I was sure would be one of our finest visits together. As we arrived, the anticipation only grew. We took a seat and I ordered my favorite meal: fried shrimp. I devoured every delicious bite, licking my fingers of each delectable crumb.

Besides feeling full and satisfied after he took me home, I don't recall anything out of the ordinary—at least my "ordinary"—that stuck out. It was all good.

Later that night, I heard my mother's voice rising, cursing at my dad over the phone. By the volume and intensity, I knew they must be arguing about something critical, something well worth yelling about. After the call ended, my mother informed me that my dad had blamed her for my shameful dining etiquette. My dad said I embarrassed him at the restaurant.

He just couldn't let anything get by him. Nothing. What I thought was an enjoyable dinner out with my father was suddenly one more thing I did wrong. Always a burden, not living up to his expectations, never good enough. And that was only one of many experiences that not only hurt me deeply but hardened my heart as well.

The little things add up over time.

Thinking about it now, it really angers me. How can a father blame a single mother for not teaching his son how to be an accomplished man? This is exactly why our boys stay angry and disengaged, lack focus, and are easily misguided. Men expect boys to act like men, but there's rarely a man in their lives patiently teaching them how to be one! In other words, like my favorite movie, *The Matrix*, everyone wants a Neo, but only a few dare to be Morpheus.

Instead of leaning on my mom's encouragement, I spent my time—what little I had with him—attempting to build a bridge to my father's unreliable love. On Saturdays, I worked at his barbershop, sweeping up hair just to be near him. The risk of hearing one more derogatory comment or feeling his dismissive glance brush over me was actually worth it.

There's just something irresistible about hope.

Even when things at times convince you it's all a hoax. Such as on days my father went out of his way to squash it. Once, he asked me to turn on the air-conditioning without showing me how the unit worked. I accidentally engaged the heat.

His response was immediate. "You dumb [expletive]!" he yelled in front of everyone. "Move out of the way!" A deadly quiet fell over the shop. All I could do was sit down and drop my head in disgrace.

Aggressively yelling at a boy is as effective as attempting to stitch up a wound with a needle and no suture. Discipline without love is ineffectual.

I don't know whether it was his own conviction for treating me badly or whether one of his customers called him out for it, but he apologized that night and gave me *fifty* dollars. I wanted to tell him that money may be a man's way of making things right, but it doesn't do a thing to heal a child's broken heart. Of course, I instantly forgave him—like a faithful dog that wags his tail after his master scolds him and sends him to the doghouse.

I just wanted to be loved by my dad, and I wanted to hear him say it.

Yet his endless negativity and disapproval hammered away at my self-esteem as my young-adult years rapidly approached.

———— • ————

In 1981 Sinclair took me to the park just up the street. The weather report didn't forecast anything falling out of the sky, but a bomb landed on me full force. My brother was moving to Texas for a better job. The economy had tanked through the 1970s energy crisis, then continued through the recession in the 1980s. The auto plants were hemorrhaging jobs, and the ripple effect traveled outward until it reached everyone.

I couldn't image life without Sinclair. All I wanted to do was curl up and cry, but that was unthinkable in my neighborhood. Crying was like a front-page advertisement for helplessness, and you'd rather be found dead than crying. It was like losing my father all over again. By the age of eleven, I was encased in a protective barrier that neither mind nor matter could breach. Instead of shedding tears, I swallowed every emotion that had the audacity to surface. I thought that at some point, becoming a man *had* to get easier.

But what did "being a man" look like?

Enter Mr. Alfred Crum, a deacon at the church we attended. My mother and he began dating, as they shared interests, their greatest being the love of the Lord. He was a solid male authority figure, and after their courtship, they married in 1982. With a thick country accent and wearing his distinctive white V-neck undershirt, jeans, and gym shoes, Mr. Crum was a good man with a strong work ethic. He was the first to teach me how to catch a baseball and a football. Still, the longing for my father continued to pound in my chest—perhaps that organ circulating blood—and because of it, accepting Mr. Crum's love would prove difficult.

After a decade of men coming and going, loving and hating, encouraging and berating, I had barricaded myself in an invisible yet impenetrable fortress—walls of defense that seemed to go up automatically, brick by tedious brick, until one day I was sealed inside. Alone.

Walls. The great escape—within the prison of my own making.

5

THE ABSENCE OF AFFIRMATION

*When our hearts are filled with security and trust in a dad
who is present and loves us, we transition from living for our
father's approval, and begin to live from his approval.*

Ed Tandy McGlasson, *The Father You've Always Wanted*

How many black men have found their strength in sports out of necessity because of a muted voice?

Since the game was first played in the 1800s, football has had a way of turning a nondescript, average boy on campus into a bona fide celebrity. Sports personalities have always held special significance for us. We affectionately lift them up to star status along with movie actors and recording artists. Their physical strength and clutch plays have drawn black men to idolize them since the great Jackie Robinson and Joe Louis.

Martial arts had the same appeal. Guys like Bruce Lee, Chuck Norris, and Jim Kelly defied gravity, effortlessly floating through air until suddenly exploding with enough power to cut down an opponent twice their size. A controlled detonation perfected and taught by an expert, an older man—a sensei. Dedicated instruction by a mentor in the ways of warriorhood could send a young man hurling past his juvenile inadequacies straight into a reputation of empowerment and respect. And the dominating martial art of the eighties was without question ninjutsu.

Ninjutsu intrigued me, and for now, I practiced alone every day. For the time being, *Black Belt* magazine would be my sensei.

Quentin was a close friend, and in the summer of 1983, he was eager to try out for a city league football team called the Detroit Cobras. I admired his enthusiasm and admit that in the past I had considered giving it a shot. Now, after working out regularly with my stepfather, Mr. Crum, and with Quentin's encouragement, I finally had the confidence to try.

On the day of tryouts, Quentin and I ran the drills with the rest of the guys—the newcomers as well as the previous year's established players. The coaches tested us on offense, defense, passing, catching, speed, and agility. The excitement on the field was contagious, lighting a fire within me.

I expected my friend to do well, but I surprised everyone with my athleticism. As it turns out, I was good—*very good*. We both made the team, and I was assigned to the starting receiver position. It was the first time I can remember feeling as if I knew who I was. I was a football player! Pride in myself had an unusual effect. It gave me worth—an invisible currency that gave me value. My father had to see me in action.

There was no ignoring me now.

I was no longer Big O's baby boy but a young man with skills that others admired and relied on. What would my dad think when he watched me on the field, dressed in my uniform, physically bigger, faster, and making the clutch plays? The thought was intoxicating. With the attention of students and coaches on me, I was ready to break out and make a statement. The stage was set.

Is it at all surprising that my dad didn't see it that way?

No matter how many times I invited him, he rarely attended my games. In my mind, I was still a second-class citizen to him, a child who demanded his costly time, an embarrassment that couldn't compete with my father's agenda. We shared the same DNA—what more did he want? And why did I care so much? Mr. Crum lived in my home and often attended my games. That should have been enough.

But it wasn't.

Despite my father and brothers' absences, I eventually relaxed into my own skin. Life was fine at Precious Blood Junior High. Friends were plentiful, and the girls thought I was cute, although they were still somewhat of a mystery. Some stole shy glances, while others whispered as I walked by. And there's always the one—every school has her—the girl whose forwardness borders on the obscene. But with a nod and a smirk, I had managed to avoid awkward conversations about sex as well as intimidating dares from classmates. All to perpetuate the illusion—to conceal one dreadful secret: I was an undercover virgin.

If growing up in your neighborhood was kinder to you—that is, if you're not lying—then you're lucky. But for boys in my community, they *sacrificed* virgins. Eighth-grade conversation sounded like a college fraternity, as disturbing as that thought is now that I have a young son of my own. Plenty of boys claiming to be sexually active were vocal about it, pressuring those of us on a steeper learning curve to take shelter behind convincing smoke screens. The braggers and attention seekers described multiple encounters with more than one girl. Like their sex lives were an open invite where every girl showed up.

But the thought of having more than one girl was foreign to me. And at such a young age, even one was too many. I wasn't ready for a real flesh-and-blood female, but there was an alternative.

A very *hands-on* approach.

Forgive my candor, but we're all men here. Without male guidance through the turbulence of testosterone surges and centerfold attractions, desperate times require desperate measures—namely stealing X-rated magazines. The gamble of getting caught and arrested far outweighed the hazards of revealing such a degrading lack of personal experience. I can speak only for myself, but as a boy, masturbation was my only option for a relationship with a girl without getting my feelings hurt. I was in control of my uncontrollable urges.

Unbeknownst to me, the simple act of masturbating (along with a creative fantasy life) was a gateway drug. It's a doorway that Satan monitors around the clock, looking for vulnerable people with a weakness for their own imagination. A beautiful naked girl—a playmate in glossy full-spectrum color—and suddenly you have an uncontrollable desire to see her walking, talking, interacting, and doing things that you guard with your life within the privacy of your own mind. Pornography—a drug by definition because of its highly addictive nature.

Even if you don't choose to see it that way, it doesn't really matter. The habit and consequences still remain. The compulsion to eat the fruit is something we've been fighting since that fateful day in the garden. It's an impulse that has been baked into us generation after generation since Adam took that first bite. Satan was there then, and he's here now, still feeding off our carnal craving for flesh and control.

To make things worse, I could grow a respectable mustache at the age of thirteen. It was a convincing fake ID when renting X-rated movies from the neighborhood video store. My mother never knew; I'm sure she was clueless as to why I asked her to buy the video of Prince's movie *Purple Rain*. How many times did I rewind it to the scene where Apollonia walks topless out of the lake? How many times did you?

Habit and consequence. The tendency took hold, and suddenly my focus and priorities shifted from good grades to "gettin' some." Like two magnets unable to resist each other, those sexual images dragged me in. The high was so distracting—at times demanding—that it took zero contemplating. All I had to do was react. And, brother, did I ever react.

There were even a few opportunities when I could have replaced the image with a live girl, but I didn't—I *couldn't*. To say I was conflicted about sex is putting it mildly.

I blame it on Sinclair and his radical conversion to Christianity and demonstration of human holiness with its resistance to worldly compromise. An outward pledge of chastity would be met only by unrelenting jokes and laughter from my boys. Where was that elusive male figure—the sane voice of adult reason—that might tell me it was not only acceptable but also sensible to save my virginity until marriage?

There's a reason King Solomon advised his sons to "drink water from your *own* well—share your love only with your wife. Why spill the water [sperm] of your springs in the streets, having sex with just anyone?… Why be captivated, my son, by an immoral woman, or fondle the breasts of a promiscuous woman?" (Prov. 5:15–16, 20).

Words of wisdom from one very experienced man to his young-adult sons. And like Solomon, I encourage the young men and boys I now work with at CATTA to think twice before recklessly deserting their virginity for fleeting sexual pleasure. If you're a virgin, keep your power! If not, save your remaining power for your wife. My brothers, do not be deceived by misleading mantras, because good guys don't finish last. They finish just in time for a woman who patiently waits.

———— • ————

When that final bell rang, it was like the sharks swarmed to feed on a vulnerable school of guppies. Kids from the surrounding neighborhood could smell blood—Precious Blood. They considered us "punks" because Precious Blood Junior High was a private school that required us to wear uniforms. Somebody walking down the street always seemed to have a beef with us.

Nearly every day at 2:30 p.m., my best friend and I would take the same route to his house and pass the time until my mother got off work and could come and get me. To tell you the truth, it seemed as if every day someone was trying to rob us of our shoes or coats. Adidas Top Ten, jingle boots, and the infamous Max Julian were the popular gear of my generation. If you were wearing any of these coveted items, you could expect to hear the words, "Check it in!" That meant you had three options: (1) hand over what they wanted, (2) run for your life, or (3) turn and fight.

If they were "crewed up," you'd get beat down. If they were strapped, you'd get shot. That's just the way it was. The hardest survived, and the rest, God willing, recovered.

Hypervigilance is exhausting at any age, and at my school, we were genuinely tired of being harassed. The confrontation came to a head when some boys from a neighboring school boldly posted up to our premises, and within minutes a brawl erupted. Violent blows were thrown with fists and nunchucks—a notorious martial art weapon—drawing the principal into the conflict but to no avail. Eventually enough administrative staff defused the clash, but the hatred remained.

———— • ————

The year went on, and the Cobras football team won critical games, moving us up in the league's rankings. As the playoffs approached, the matchup against our long-standing rival, the Cougars, was a game we all had anticipated for weeks. This would determine the championship, which we were bound to be playing in—after winning the game at hand.

Nervous energy had me and my teammates pacing in front of stands packed to capacity with parents, teachers, and students, as well as a certain cheerleader—one that I'd had my eye on for some time. An opportune moment, to say the least.

It would be impossible to ignore me if I was the biggest wide receiver on the field. Opponents, coaches, and the pretty cheerleader—especially the cheerleader—couldn't deny my presence. Having anticipated this moment the week prior, I begged my mother to buy linebacker shoulder pads for me so I would look broader.

Suddenly I was strapping on the oversize equipment and suiting up. The shoulder pads were significantly wider than my shoulders, but I was sure I still had the range of motion to play well. If all went as planned, this would be the game that would catapult me to citywide celebrity.

My team ran onto the field as the swell of cheers convinced me that this was actually my life!

With adrenaline coursing through my developing adolescent body, the coming playoffs wasn't the only thing weighing on me. It was the linebacker's mammoth pads—bulky and unruly—that protruded from my slim physique. They felt clumsy and awkward, but I played a good game and even made a few blocks that my coach couldn't believe.

With the score tied and time short, it was a made-for-TV movie climax when a collective breath is held by the crowd as that all-important final clutch play unfolds. A history-making moment created by the likes of Hank Aaron, Muhammad Ali, Walter Payton, and ... *Jason Wilson*. As we settled onto the line of scrimmage, our quarterback, Shonté Fleming, began his cadence—a route we had practiced a hundred times before. *This was going to be good!* At the snap, the blitz came and I took off. Shonté threw the perfect spiral. It spun on a thread, descending toward me in a textbook pass.

It couldn't get any better than this. I felt as if the world was watching.

The ball spiraled effortlessly …

Hit my enormous shoulder pads …

And bounced off as the clock ran out.

I stood motionless for a second as the game buzzer sounded, in shock that I had dropped such a makeable catch. We lost. We lost because of *me*.

When I looked up, the excruciating disappointment and disbelief written on the faces of my teammates were mocked by the celebration exploding on the opposite side of the field. I felt lifeless as I climbed the bleachers—a lesson in humility I could have used sooner.

It wasn't ego, and it wasn't vanity. It was pure lack of self-esteem that drove me to pretend I was bigger than I actually was. Bigger, badder, tougher … all the things that go with being a stereotypical male. They're drilled into us from the day we're born, filling a mold—the metal backbone of steel designed to withstand the pressure, the threat of human tears and lost virility.

And of all the games for my father to attend, it had to be this one.

"I heard you dropped a touchdown pass" was the first thing out of his mouth. Not "Great catch in the first quarter" or "That block on fifty-seven was legit!" Just the same predictable negativity that refused to see the good in me. I didn't respond. What was there to say?

Would you believe it took nearly three decades for the Most High to expose what my dad really said?

"I *heard* ..."

I missed its meaning the first time.

He didn't even see the play because he wasn't there. He showed up at the end of the game. He didn't witness anything I did—good or bad. The speed I used to outpace my competitor, the great plays I participated in, or the joy I had doing the thing I was truly gifted at. Nothing. Just a handful of corrosive words hitting me like acid. He could have said so much, but all he did say was "I *heard* ..."

Sitting here in my office so many years later, I finally realized what he actually meant. And when I did, all I could do was put my head on my desk and cry. It makes me appreciate how the Most High allows us the time—years—to prepare for yesterday's pain. To see it in the light of adult understanding, waiting until we're able to survive the impact. He's such a kind Father.

Beyond the humiliation of that lost football game, we did make it to the playoffs the following week. Once again, we squared off against the Cougars, but this time I wouldn't make the same mistake. This game was all about vindication!

But for three quarters, Shonté threw pass after pass, just never to me. So many times I could have easily caught it, but his eyes said, "Jay, I want to throw it to you, but I just can't."

So clear was my frustration that my stepfather, Mr. Crum, saw it from the stands. When the fourth quarter began, his patience had run its course. Defiant, he left his seat in the stands to have a word with my coach, who happened to be his friend and coworker.

Yelling into the sideline chaos, Mr. Crum shouted, "Why aren't you throwing the ball to my son? Come on, man, he's wide open!"

Friendship is a beautiful thing.

With better judgment prevailing and Mr. Crum's animated persuasion assailing, Coach signaled to Shonté to go ahead and throw me a pass. And as the ball went up, so did my stock as I came down with it—good for a first down. The magic was back! We quickly reestablished all the routes that delivered so many victories in the past. But even the touchdown I scored in the final minutes wasn't enough.

We lost the game, and I cried all the way home.

The only saving grace was that my father wasn't there to see it. His work at the barbershop was more important than the big playoff game any other dad wouldn't have missed. And even though I was secretly relieved he wasn't there to witness my coach's lack of trust, any residue of faith in myself had vanished. From that point on, I refused to believe in myself.

Life was too short, and my skin was too thin.

6

TRAUMA AND THE BLACK EXPERIENCE

The paradox of trauma is that it has both the power to
destroy and the power to transform and resurrect.

Peter A. Levine, PhD, *In an Unspoken Voice*

An internal hum, an uneasy vibration that rattles nerve endings just below the surface of your skin.

It was the last day of school before Easter break in April of 1984. Class started the way it always did, with students running to take their seats before the final bell. The atmosphere was easy in both eighth-grade homerooms. Since it was only a half day, the teachers let us play games and chill with our friends.

Just another day in the life of a Detroit thirteen-year-old.

It wasn't a secret that the gang running the surrounding neighborhood had plans to jump us after school. It was common practice to stay alert, prepared for anything during those walks home through unfriendly territory, but today was different. Tension had been escalating for weeks, and that afternoon was tagged for confrontation. We all had to be ready to protect ourselves.

Off the radar from the school administration, a few eighth graders had brought guns to school. There comes a point when fists, bottles, bats, and anything else just aren't enough. And no calling a truce—negotiating was another sign of weakness. The battle lines had been drawn. Words were exchanged. Weapons in hand.

I admit I had contemplated bringing my stepfather's gun but decided against it. At the time, I wasn't comfortable with the thought of causing bodily harm to someone, but I could never admit it. No boy could.

Kelly was a friend who shared my love of music. We would talk about our favorite songs, and classmates and I would sing André Cymone's hit "Kelly's Eyes" to her, on account of her beautiful eyes. She had a sweet spirit and fun nature that made her easy to be around.

She and other friends were down the hall in their own eighth-grade homeroom, counting off the minutes before vacation officially began. That also meant getting mentally primed for the risky walk home. A student was showing off his .25 caliber semiautomatic handgun. As covert as young boys can be, responsibility is often fleeting. He removed the clip from the gun. Then a loud *bang*!

The class turned around and their faces froze in shock. The teacher thought the loud sound was a firecracker. But it was the screams following the blast that confirmed something much worse had happened.

"I don't know what happened … it just went off. It just went off!"

From my classroom next door, we heard an army of footsteps running into the hallway, and we assumed a fight had broken out. Rushing out excitedly to see who was winning, we found a fight in progress—a little girl fighting for her life. My sweet friend Kelly was slumped over backward in her chair …

Shot in the head.

Classmates were crying as teachers ran in. My godbrother Gabriel looked me square in the eyes.

"Kelly got shot."

The air in my lungs vanished, and my arms felt numb. The idea that she had taken a bullet was unimaginable. Her helpless young body drooped like a rag doll, unconscious in the next room, and there was nothing I could do about it. The classroom was cleared as the paramedics arrived. They tried desperately to save Kelly's life, and though the hospital was only blocks from there, Kelly slipped away—reportedly within minutes.

The police search and seizure unearthed a total of three guns and two knives.

As we filed out of the school, stunned and distraught, I saw Kelly's mother, Ms. Audrey, sitting in her car. She had just been told that her baby wouldn't be coming home. Hysterical, she was banging her head against the steering wheel, consumed by the same despair and anger I had seen years before. Her tears exhumed memories of my own mother's devastation when told she had lost her child.

Climbing into Mama's car, a strange sense of survivor's guilt washed over me. Ms. Audrey would never again hear Kelly singing to the radio beside her. There would be no daughter in the pretty

Easter dress that hung in the closet—the price tag forever attached. No more memories made.

Just a steering wheel taking the brunt of a mother's unbearable grief.

When my mom and I got home, we watched the news report that played on a loop, adding more disturbing details each time around. I was still numb and stoic. That internal hum, an uneasy vibration that rattles nerve endings just below the surface. I went outside for air and started throwing my ninja shurikens (sharp star-shaped weapons).

Each one hit the tree, sticking to its bark, stabbing, slicing. It cleared my mind and gave me something else to focus on. A way to redirect my anger. Another life gone. Kelly … she never caused any trouble. She was the last person I could imagine this happening to.

Another day in the life—and death—of a Detroit thirteen-year-old.

Why is it that though this experience was one of the most traumatic of my life, I can hardly remember the details of the funeral? Yah being kind again, shielding me from things too piercing and painful. However, one of the few things I do recall is the pastor of the church. He was a gentle yet strong man doing his best to console everyone to little avail. The sorrow in that room, the exposed raw emotion—it was like being buried alive. The shallowest breath pulling worn heartstrings nearly to their breaking point.

But this pastor—this man of faith—made an impression. Little did I know that he would eventually become my father-in-law. That my future wife, his eleven-year-old daughter, Nicole, was sitting just rows from me. Now, as I type this, I consider my own mother as she sat through yet another memorial service for someone so young, a decade after losing Larry. When would it all stop? Would it *ever* stop?

Though Mama paid for me to attend a private school, hoping for a better education and a safe space amid the turmoil of Detroit, death was just down the hall.

It was the first fatal school shooting of a student in Detroit's history. But unlike today, no counselors were dispatched to help grieving students, no therapy dogs or rallies or candlelight vigils. As a result, I developed the symptoms of what is now diagnosed as acute stress disorder (ASD). Honestly, I cannot remember whether I even cried at Kelly's funeral. I was in shock and no one knew it. I swallowed my emotions as my heart became a reservoir of sorrow and anger.

Trauma—was it just a part of the black experience?

7

THE PRESSURE OF PROMISCUITY

Promiscuity is like never reading past the first page.

Mason Cooley

When one young life is lost, a hundred more are left to struggle to find a reason.

After the horrific death of my dear friend Kelly, what small scraps of security left in me were protected within a thick outer casing of cynicism. My heart was being held together by my friends who remained. Precious Blood Junior High was in mourning for the rest of that school year.

There we stood, fourteen years old and eager to be moving up into high school the following fall. Graduation of any kind is something you always remember—the excited expressions of your classmates, proud teachers, family members who were there and those who *weren't*.

"Boy, I will come to the *real* graduation!"

Whether a playoff game or a milestone, my dad was MIA. I had seen him miss work for something as trivial as a bowling tournament. I guess my junior high graduation was less than that. I started to believe that nothing I did would ever warrant his precious time or approval. Making money meant more to him than making his son feel loved.

Another failed attempt to interrupt what was an ever-growing string of letdowns that featured me and the inevitable empty chair in the room. Another "special day" made blatantly ordinary. Round and round it went, like the vinyl on my mother's massive wood stereo system in our living room.

With summer in full swing, it brought more time for my newly discovered passion—deejaying. I don't know how many of Mama's records I ruined learning how to scratch. All I know is that it felt like art. Spinning and scratching, learning and creating, remembering and *forgetting*.

In 1984 we took a trip to Fort Lauderdale, Florida, to visit family. My favorite cousin, Kevin, was another male figure who held my attention. Being eighteen years old and an athlete, it was easy to admire him. He hung with all the coolest guys and the prettiest girls.

The trip couldn't have come at a better time with a citywide event called Playday about to commence. It spotlighted all the hottest DJs and artists from near and far. It meant I would finally experience the legendary Jam Pony Express DJs!

Coming from the north, this was also my first time hearing the words "my nigga" spoken as a term of endearment among young black men. I couldn't get comfortable with the phrase. Its root was historically derogatory and a description that in no way reflected the respect and beauty the African American ethnicity deserved.

After taking in the tsunami of sound that was Playday, Kevin and I retreated to his girlfriend's house to chill. Her sister was about my age and, oh, so cute. When Kevin introduced us, sparks flew in my direction, but I was too shy to feed the flame or the conversation. And when Kevin and his girlfriend slipped from the room, any fire remaining was awkwardly extinguished. Still, we smiled, talked, and flirted.

Disaster averted.

Yes, I had kissed girls before. But I didn't have the confidence it took to kiss one I had just met, much less make a move sexually. My virginity was still well intact, and it wasn't something I was willing to simply throw away. To be honest, it wasn't even something I thought about a lot. All I knew was that the time and person had to be right.

About thirty minutes later, Kevin came back in, and we left.

It was during the car ride home that he started to grill me. "So you get some?"

Please, not this again! I was hoping this tiresome game of Twenty Questions had been left in the halls of Precious Blood. I reluctantly told him I hadn't. Then he pressed, asking me whether I at least kissed her and got my "freak on." Again, I told him no. But he just wouldn't let it go.

"Cuz, you never got none?" he continued.

"No!" I answered, totally embarrassed.

There it was—called out by my favorite, cool cousin. I wondered what my chances were of staying in his good graces now that he knew the unbearable truth. But it was too late to backtrack. I sat in silence for what had to be the longest car ride of my life.

When we finally pulled up to our uncle's house, the entire family was gathered inside. It took less than a nanosecond for Kevin to yell out as we stepped through the front door.

"Hey, y'all, did y'all know Jason's never had sex?"

I was mortified.

It was one of those moments when you would give anything to be invisible—to be nothing was infinitely better than this. Thunderous laughter echoed throughout the house, followed by what had to be the single most humiliating experience of my life. Even after years of emotional cement mixing, concrete pouring, and fortress building, the defenses built around my heart were still demolished in an instant and by those closest to me.

Why couldn't I be unshakable, unbreakable—a grown man?

Chuckling along with them, I tried to hide my humiliation. But seeing right through me, they laughed even louder. I was the joke of the century, and no amount of phony denial or submissive humor could save me. It was a full-on frontal attack on my dignity.

I frantically skimmed the amused faces in the room, looking for the support of my mother, only to find her laughing at me along with everybody else. In my family's eyes, a fourteen-year-old boy should have had sex by now, and my lack of experience made me pathetic.

Trauma … it's not always physical. I think emotional pain can often do far more damage. Many times bodily scars heal almost as good as new. A hairline scar or bruised tissue can easily be overlooked. But it's the mental wounds that dig the deepest, rip the lining of our hope, and hinder our healing.

The pressure to become sexually active, and the shame and guilt that went with it, left me changed. I made a decision right then and there: I was going to have sex, and soon, if only to gain the respect I needed to escape future ridicule and survive high school. I turned fourteen that August and felt that my masculinity had already been assaulted. It was up to me to establish my manliness as I entered my first year at Benedictine High School. As I think back on that part of my life—the need to sleep with a girl just to make a social declaration of manhood—I regret that decision to this day.

Unfortunately, I still allowed misconstrued masculinity to influence me. My freshman year took a turn for the worse when my first attempt at selling marijuana went bad. The weed I had purchased turned out to be less than legit. By the time a friend informed me, my entire supply had been sold. What kind of drug dealer doesn't test his product first? But I wasn't a "dealer," just a young man in desperate need of affirmation.

Rumors swirled, quickly followed by threats. I knew I had some explaining to do. But since I wasn't known for being shady, the conflict was resolved quickly, and I emerged unscathed. When a young man knows why he exists, he will no longer risk his existence. But sadly, my father wasn't around to show me my purpose, but my heavenly Father was still there.

But from grades to attitude, I was bottoming out.

Gone were the days of peer approval and popularity. Somewhere along the way, between hormone fluxes and centerfold playmates, I became detached and indifferent. Like countless African American boys today, my will was slowly draining out of me. Where was joy? Where was hope? Where was I?

I had only one interest left. And in hindsight, it's what kept my world turning.

After seeing the renowned Jam Master Jay in concert, I dove headlong into my preferred art form—the only one that made sense out of anything—deejaying.

This relatively new art form required equipment, and not the kind you find in a secondhand store. I mean expensive equipment. My father's backing wasn't an option, even though his income exceeded Mama's. God bless my mother for the sacrifice she made, buying the very best turntables available.

Now all I needed was a mixer to connect the two turntables. My stepmother, Ann, who was my father's third wife and the mother of my beloved little sister, Olivia, wanted to help. So she bought me a kitchen blender. After a few laughs about mixing fruit, she went out and bought the correct equipment.

Sacrifices have a way of putting things back into place, sometimes where they were always meant to be. A very personal and purposeful act with the ability to release the past while holding the keys to the future can change everything.

Three hours a day, seven days a week I practiced. Some said that I was becoming one of the best DJs in Detroit, and my growing fan base agreed. The next year of high school brought with it monetary success that far exceeded that of average teenagers in the eighties, generating about eight hundred dollars each month in mixtape sales and parties I deejayed.

I was no longer being overlooked.

Several rappers in the hood acknowledged my work, and I was soon given the name "Mystro" for the way I moved a crowd. I had found my identity, just not the identity the Most High had in mind. Yah had given me the gift of exhortation, but I was using it to create an atmosphere for drugs, alcohol abuse, and premarital sex. I was the maestro all right—for Satan's orchestra as he wrote each verse and arranged every composition. I held the baton while he pulled the strings. A puppet he used to manipulate and sway people toward him.

I'm not putting all the blame on the Devil. After all, I was there too. But how blind we are when the Enemy appeals to our vanity. Satan was heaven's number one musician until his love of self, his own beauty, and his desire to be "the man" took him down. A lesson we can all learn. That much love and affirmation can blind us to the truth, as it did me. I lost sight of everything: my education, honoring my mother, Yah's plan.

Mama would stay up worrying, anxiously waiting for me to make it home after each party. Like most teenagers, I was self-absorbed with tunnel vision. I never considered the role that my brother's death played in her overreaching protection. To me, it was irritating and unnecessary, even on the nights gangs brawled or gunplay erupted.

Music, my boys, and the girls ... in that order. It was this short-sighted priority list that eventually had to right itself. And when that fateful day came—the one I had waited for and dreaded at the same time—I still wasn't ready.

———— • ————

Yes, she was pretty. Every curve of her body made for a beautiful picture. I just wasn't feeling her. Gabriel, my friend and godbrother, slid next to me with his classic devilish grin.

"Jay, she wants to [expletive] you."

This was exactly what I was trying to avoid.

"I don't have a rubber," I said, hoping for a way out.

Gabe quickly took a condom out of his pocket as if to say, "No worries, bro. I got you." He may have been my age, but he never showed up unprepared. He carried them like a piece of gear they issue when you enter the military.

Was this it? My youthful ideals about waiting for the right girl seemed so far away. And the little boy who held so tightly to them suddenly vanished along with any recourse I had left.

Virginity was a disgrace. At least that's what negative peer pressure decreed. And I would never have peace until I got a *piece*. I took the condom from Gabe and motioned to her. We met downstairs in the basement.

She was a couple of years older and knew how to handle herself. This wasn't her first time in the boxing ring—no cornermen required. Just her hands and body blows. Before I knew it, I had lost my virginity to someone I didn't have feelings for. The act of sex was even cheaper than I had realized. Mere minutes of her self-gratification, then ... *nothing*. Just a sick sense of hype letdown.

My boys were all upstairs listening to the pounding of bodies.

When I reemerged, holding that invisible yet coveted championship belt (the one I never asked for), their tight-lipped smirks announced the winner. But their pride in me was wasted. I didn't want their approval for something I felt obligated to give them. I had compromised my own moral code to satisfy a bunch of guys that at some point had been pressured into doing the same. The cycle remained unbroken.

They didn't understand the gravity of what had just taken place— that something priceless had been taken from me. And I wasn't about to tell them. For all they knew, this was one more notch in my belt, one more time in the ring. But it was during the drive home that it became real.

I had changed.

Between the time I showed up at Gabe's house and the time I left, those minutes spent in the basement changed me into a different person. I was relieved that it was over but disgusted for having caved to the pressure of the crowd.

Then I thought about the girl—how nice she was to me—and I felt bad for her. By having sex with me, she believed I would fall in love with her. Instead, I don't remember ever seeing her again. Love ... in a basement. Can you imagine?

Any innocence in me an hour before was gone. Not by force, but by resignation. Along with the burden of hiding something as unacceptable as virtue, the threads of decency and respect for women finally broke.

I was free from the expectations of morality.

The transformation of my attitude and actions was immediate. Instead of treating girls with the regard their gender deserved, I used derogatory names and threw shade when they upset or rejected me. In my eyes, they didn't look the same. Even my mother.

Sex should come with a disclaimer for anyone not married. And depending on what that first experience is—whether consensual, positive, and loving or forced, superficial, and reflexive—it introduces you to the best part of you or the worst part of you.

An X-rated magazine, porn movie, or naked female in the flesh—those are all images committed to your memory, for better or worse.

However, when you unite with a woman who is not your wife, you "sin against your own body" (1 Cor. 6:18). Could you imagine being in a boxing match and every time you hit your opponent, you feel the punch? My brothers, this is what happens when we misuse women to fulfill the need for affirmation. We must learn to live from who we are instead of what we do.

The alteration of my conduct was alarming. And as I changed, my friends did as well. The Mystro—dominant centerpiece of some of the best Detroit parties—was now drinking forty-ounce beers and acting recklessly. How could someone so young feel so old? I was treating my mother audaciously, talking back or altogether ignoring her as I paraded around, acting like the man of the house. When my stepfather tried to intervene, my mom wouldn't allow it. She refused to let Mr. Crum discipline me, and by doing so did more harm than good. It only enabled me to continue on a path of destruction.

Eventually this resulted in a wedge developing between my mom and my stepdad, affecting their relationship. My grades continued to drop, but with the crutch of college nowhere in my future, I completed just enough schoolwork to keep me from failing.

My inspiration was music. My lust was for sex. My love was for money.

Promiscuity has many faces, all with the power to hijack our loyalty. It compromises our view, pressures us to rethink sound judgment, and tends to lean with the dim majority. It can build slowly over time or intimidate in an instant. It's a device—a tactic—Satan uses to beguile our souls, sending us deeper into the wilderness of self-indulgence.

The pressures of promiscuity pushed a bargaining chip across the table, daring me.

And impulsively, I picked it up.

8

A BOXER WITHOUT A CORNER

The greatest battle will be discovering how to not fight old battles.

Grandmaster Charles Allen

I wasn't "hood," but I looked hood, so the hood would test my *hood,* and I foolishly let it.

B&E—breaking and entering—took me and some boys to a house one afternoon that we had every intention of burglarizing. We rang the doorbell—the accepted strategy used when casing a crib—and being my first time, it was all new. It seemed I was finding my way to the first for a lot of things.

Footsteps inside methodically made their way to the front door. When it opened, we asked for so-and-so, a made-up name to cover the truth; then we took off. Let's call it divine intervention that the homeowner was there, ultimately saving me from actually committing a crime. But the push and pull of my corruptible side continued to challenge the good in me. There was light in my heart, but the shade covering it came from the company I was keeping. And for B&E jobs, any sort of light tends to work against you. The same can be said for all shady deeds—douse the light!

The last thing I wanted to do was disappoint my boys. And after disappointing my dad for years, this was an opportunity to please the male figures around me.

Divine intervention—oh, the irony.

I wasn't Catholic, but then you didn't have to be to attend Benedictine. Private Catholic schools were big in 1980s Detroit, and though my freshman year at "Bene" could have taken a turn for the worse after my first drug deal, my tenth-grade year began well. New friends, beautiful girls. Everything was good. Everything but the rule book that was set in stone like army regulations. And there was one rule in particular that offended this boy who learned to shave by the seventh grade out of necessity. No beards!

But how offensive could a short goatee possibly be? Cropped nice and close under my chin, they would never see it. Unfortunately, nuns must have holy radar. Sisters are notorious for wielding wooden yardsticks, smacking knuckles, and lording over students by intimidation. And the nun who spotted my fringe came at me like a woman on a mission.

Pulling my chin, she yelled, "What is this?"

I admit she caught me off guard, and my reflexes jumped in, slapping her hand away. All that unresolved anger astonished her as she inhaled with her mouth and eyes wide open. Grabbing my arm good and tight, she dragged me to the principal's office as a defector before the firing squad.

It was my first time in the principal's office, but like so many of my firsts, it was, if anything, predictable.

Along with my first high school suspension came a naked chin that was both degrading and embarrassing. Just when the girls were locking in, I was suddenly channeling Samson without his locks (see Judg. 16). No goatee, no game. Okay, that's not exactly true, but that's how it felt.

I was getting harder, tougher, more self-absorbed—just like my dad. It was during that tenth-grade year at Benedictine that Mama divorced Mr. Crum.

And I was the cause.

Between my selfish antics and the ongoing anxiety they created, my stepdad must have realized it was a battle he couldn't win—that, and the shotgun pointed at him. What can I say? He pushed me. During that last heated argument between them, I decided it was time for Mr. Crum to hold his tongue. I was sick of listening to any man yell at my mother. It didn't matter that he was simply trying to help her guide me out of harm's way. And when he told her I would make her cry, that sealed it.

Staring at me holding a shotgun must have brought a certain clarity, because he moved out that day—something I would later regret. After he left, she was alone to deal with me and the mounting drama that ensued.

By the end of that school year, I had lost my desire to attend Benedictine, and I transferred to Oak Park High, a popular suburban school on the outskirts of Detroit.

Moving children from one school to another was a frequent practice in the late eighties when parents were losing faith in the Detroit public school system. They sought ways for their kids to attend outlying residential schools for a better education. And in order for me to attend Oak Park, I would have to live with my aunt Lola and cousin Ivy during the week.

———— • ————

Life at Oak Park High was sweet … largely because of my boy up the block, Nate Slappey. If anyone could step into my shoes and walk around for a day, it was Nate. Since childhood, he was a part of my life. We hung out at the mall and played basketball and football. We dressed alike, thought alike, and nobody knew me as well as Nate. And wherever Nate was, I was close by, and vice versa.

Nate already had friends when I got there, so the transition was easy. Being a skilled deejay afforded me all kinds of friends, mostly among the juniors and seniors. Oak Park suited me. But pride is no small diversion. It can interrupt forward motion and steal peace.

He wasn't in my crew—the one rumored to have talked behind my back. I had to confront him. But instead of taking the time needed to process my emotions, I allowed the instigating words of a classmate to stir me into doing something I couldn't reverse. As the last bell rang, we approached each other. He was bigger and stronger, but I didn't care. Not even my "slip-n-slides" kept me from walking right over to him and mushing his glasses into his face. Before I knew what happened, he was on top of me throwing punches.

Blow after blow, they kept coming. And though I managed to avoid the brunt of the attack—showing little physical evidence of a fight—I couldn't move. I was on the ground, immobile, and unable to get up. If only I had learned Brazilian Jiujitsu by then! Nate and my boys quickly swarmed, and it escalated into an all-out brawl.

Again, I was suspended and sent home.

Without Mr. Crum there, and without Larry or Sinclair, loneliness and defeat set in. Nate was a peer, not a parental figure. And as the sun and isolation fell, my thoughts drifted back to my dad. He was the one my heart always returned to—a heart that ached a little more each time it took a hit. I needed to call him, just to talk to someone. Maybe he could relate to what I was going through and maybe care just enough to tell me it was all going to be okay.

As the phone rang, I felt hopeful. He answered, and with a lump in my throat, I confided in him, telling him everything that had happened.

"So … who won?" is all he wanted to know.

"If anything, it was a tie," I answered, "but I think I lost."

Dead silence.

Then, with his usual half-disappointed, half-impatient tone, "Look, I've got to get back to work."

And that was it. No sage advice or personal stories of vindication. No teachable moment or lesson about resilience and fortitude. He made me feel like I lost every fight I had been in—a failure.

Like a boxer without a corner with nowhere to rest, nowhere to breathe, taking jab after jab, the fighter—the survivor—in me walked out of the ring that night. With my soul pummeled and swollen, I sat alone on the floor of my room with the lights out until morning.

Suspension wasn't easy. Being an ostracized kid is never easy. Kicked out and designated outcast, some boys take the time to regret what they've done, while others grow colder every minute they're away. But one in a hundred decide to accept the label and lie down.

When I returned to school on Friday, those steps to the front door were nearly insurmountable. Like climbing Kilimanjaro, I tried to pull my feet inside the building, but I could take only a few steps. The air was just too thin. The incident was still too raw, and the only thing I could focus on was the lingering embarrassment and anger still fresh in my mind. What was I going to do? What would I say? Where could I go?

I decided to take the weekend to chill and return for a fresh start on Monday. I wandered about Oak Park to air my thoughts, then walked back to Aunt Lola's house.

My questions were soon answered for me when a teacher who was a friend of my mother informed her that the Oak Park administration was investigating the legitimacy of my address. With my residential status called into question, my mother was worried that Aunt Lola would get into trouble. To end the speculation, she pulled me out of Oak Park.

Another school I loved; another school I had to leave.

After the investigation, Nate and many others had to transfer schools. The trickle-down effect is real. We should never allow our emotions to dictate our actions, because our decisions can disrupt the lives of others.

It's difficult to relive this part of my journey—entering manhood with so much guilt, baggage, rage, and low self-esteem—and revisit how desperate and out of control I felt. Left to my own devices, I would crush a mosquito with a sledgehammer. I didn't care about the damage I caused doing it. The mosquito would be dead, and I would have nothing to feel sorry for.

If only Nate or my boys knew how badly I needed them. Just one friend to make a conscious effort to encourage me or help me through those complicated times.

Every boy needs a crew; every man needs camaraderie and a safe space to not only express his emotions but also release them, venting his cares to someone who cares. Sadly, a man's concerns are often heard as complaining, just as a dog's bark is annoying when no one sees trouble. Both warnings are rarely heeded before "the thief" breaks in and steals, kills, and destroys everything, even the dog. As men, we must take care of ourselves by truthfully expressing ourselves with other men we can trust. No matter our age, transparency will set us free.

But things look different through young eyes. When my girlfriend told me that some in my circle were cracking jokes about me, I could have sunk to the bottom. While I did forgive them, I never forgot it. How could I when I would never have played them that way? In their defense, they were high schoolers and doing the best with what they had.

So was I.

———— • ————

My next stop on the tour of Catholic high schools was Saint Martin de Porres High School. I had reached my junior year in 1987 and was wearing a full Teddy Pendergrass beard. The majority of the girls thought I was a visiting parent, which was comical! I made friends fast, and the next year the senior class was a tight group.

The hip-hop culture was evolving and gaining momentum. My favorite rappers were the ones with the hardest look and lyrics. It was rare to see a rapper smile on an album cover, with songs like "I Ain't No Joke" by Eric B. & Rakim and "Criminal Minded" by Boogie Down Productions. This made it almost impossible for a young man my age to smile without getting labeled "soft." Although I was not raised to be a thug and never desired to be one, I had to conform to the culture or be an outcast. And you couldn't just *look* tough; you had to act tough.

Pranks, antics, exploits … one after another.

Profanity written on a classroom door. Cussing at a teacher. Intruding on a class, stirring up trouble. Within hours, a friend and I were called to the office.

On the way, I mentally rehearsed my usual passive-aggressive "I didn't do nothing" demeanor. When the principal took one look at me, she refused to believe I could have done such a thing. She insisted that my boy come clean and confess. I turned to him with my faux innocence on full display. *And the Oscar goes to …* Though he didn't leave the colorful message on the classroom door, he did take the blame. That's called loyalty. In my circle, we had a pact. Whoever got busted—guilty or not—would take the fall for all. An unwritten law within a very tangible reality.

What if we could count the cost before we pay too much—before actions flare into more than a crime committed only in our minds? An imaginary offense that wasn't meant to harm. What if we could hit Pause before the crash of a mistake? What if we could erase what was about to be?

What if …

I started wearing glasses at an early age, and I was still wearing them in high school. A friend of mine, messing around, playfully smushed the frames into my face. Laughter broke out from students watching, and suddenly a violent flood of memories rushed in. Hearing those echoing ghosts in the hall, I was back at Oak Park High again, reliving the humiliation heaped on me by foes and friends alike.

Before I knew it, I had body-slammed my friend to the concrete so hard, everyone heard the impact.

A few girls looking on were stunned as one said, "Dang, why you have to do all that?"

Shaken and conflicted, I walked off as my friend lay on the ground.

I couldn't believe I did it, but then again, I could. Something in me refused to lose another fight or be the brunt of another joke. Even at the cost of losing a friend.

Now, so many years later, I see the same behavior playing out in schools and playgrounds across Metro Detroit as I work with boys through CATTA. So much pain disguised as an unbreakable defense. Pride coupled with the fear of being exposed for who they really are pressures them to fit in to a fake world that's real.

And I was no different.

But what if one day the price of my pride would be too high to pay?

9

A BROTHER FROM ANOTHER MOTHER

A friend is always loyal, and a brother is born to help in time of need.

King Solomon, Proverbs 17:17

The winter semester melted into spring, and suddenly it was the summer of 1988 and time to graduate.

Food, fun, girls, and beer. What better way to say good-bye to friends and classmates than at the highly anticipated senior cookout? I could see it—driving up in style in a white-on-white Nissan Maxima. Talks between my father and me had resumed, albeit sporadically. But I had chosen the perfect graduation gift that could make up for so much time lost—to borrow his new ride for the pregraduation celebration.

Unlike previous times when I had asked him for something, this time was different. I sensed it in his voice—the hesitation, the slightest vacillation ... just before he said no.

As a senior and his seasoned emotional punching bag, it took a lot to pull tears to my eyes, but he managed it. However, my reaction this time was swift and unforgiving.

"You've never been there for me! And I'll never ask you for anything for the rest of my life!"

That was a promise I kept.

From the day I graduated, deejaying became my world. Winning several battles and considered by many to be the best in Detroit, I was galvanized by the thought of a career in music—the props, the money, the fame. That summer, a friend approached me about being the DJ for a rapper. It was just the kind of offer I had been hoping for.

Teferi Brent, the emcee, was a fiery personality with politically charged lyrics. Initially he and I were a toxic mix, but we shared the same passion for the music we created together. That seemed to cancel out any personality conflicts we had earlier in our relationship. Within months, we'd signed a record contract with World One Records, and now "Kaos & Mystro" were officially recording our album titled *Outcast Volume 1*. It just couldn't get any better than this.

———— • ————

Texas was agreeing with Sinclair, and he was doing well for himself. Our phone calls kept us close, but his faith hit a frequency that sharply contrasted with my own. Finding the harmony and reconciling the minor notes with the major ones only confirmed what opposite life songs we were singing. My Rick James to his Winans.

After so many spiritual conversations and hearing that same peculiar conviction in his voice, I soon stopped reaching out to Sinclair altogether. All he wanted was to see his little brother abiding in Christ. All I wanted was to romanticize Larry's fiercely free approach to living, while forgetting that it ultimately killed him. Subconsciously, his memory was being posthumously honored and gravely echoed.

Letters from Sinclair were laced with his love for Yahushua, and everything he mailed me had a Bible verse on it. It doesn't matter if it was about oxygen, Sinclair would find a way to incorporate Scripture. Still, I was too immersed in my music and making money to find any value in the gospel.

If you had "good news," it had better be about making music or selling albums—that was the gospel according to *me*. The darkness of yesterday and its menacing shadows were behind me. I was the author of my own story line—action, climax, and payoff that would be unequaled in hip-hop. It was all in my grasp, and I was holding on with both hands. Nothing was going to stop me from accomplishing my dream.

———— • ————

It happened at Blackstone, a barbershop where my father had previously cut hair. Prince was the owner and an old friend of my dad. As we talked, laughed, and reminisced about old times, his expression suddenly turned serious.

"Jason," he said, "you have a brother."

"Yes, I know. He lives in Texas," I replied, as if somehow the memory of Sinclair had escaped him.

"No, you have one in Detroit, and his name is Keith. You two were purposefully kept apart."

Why didn't that idea catch me off guard? You'd think it would have, but it didn't. My father reminded me of the Temptations song "Papa Was a Rolling Stone" ... you know the rest.

"Keith knows about you and really wants to meet you." Prince handed me a slip of paper. Another character—a twist in the plot—had been written into the narrative.

It wasn't a secret that my mother's divorce from my dad was because of an affair. But as I stared down at the phone number, I didn't put the two together, not yet. The only thought racing through my mind was that I had found another intriguing piece to my family puzzle as the genetic plot thickened.

I have a big brother, and he wants to see me!

It was in the parking lot of a drugstore when I first met Keith. He rolled up in an inconspicuous, full-size Chevy pickup with an incredible sound system. As I climbed in and sat beside him, the first thing I noticed was his demeanor—similar mannerisms and ways about us—and I knew we shared at least a few strands of the same DNA.

The second thing I noticed was that he was rich, and it didn't take a genius to figure out what his chosen profession was or the danger it involved. The drug scene in Detroit during the late eighties and early nineties was widespread and gave Keith the resources to lavish gifts on himself and others. My first car—an Isuzu Amigo truck—came out of his back pocket in cash. There was only one other like it in the city, and it belonged to a friend of mine. Such things made an impression in an environment where young men with designer brands projected power and mystique.

Keith's attempts to find me had always come up short, as he was never told where I was. But when we met, it was as if we'd known each other forever. I was hopeful that *forever* was going to last a long time.

In the months that followed, we spent nearly every day together. The glamour (for lack of a better word) of what he did was enticing, and I pressed him to involve me in every aspect of his business. The idea wasn't something he was open to. He let me count money, but that was it. When it came to the heavy drug game, he refused to let me in. He had already lost a brother to violence—and he wasn't about to potentially lose another.

Keith was a good brother, but his surroundings and situation never allowed us to develop the closer connection I so desperately wanted. I wasn't the only one wounded by our father. There was plenty of pain to go around. The same disappointments. The same selfish motivations that provoked Oliver to repeat the cycle.

When Keith was younger, he asked our dad to buy him some gym shoes—the coolest shoes every kid in Detroit wanted, Adidas Top Tens, with a price tag of eighty-five dollars. Back then, that was a lot of money for some sneakers. But though Oliver was making good money, he gave Keith only fifteen dollars. Of course he was hurt. It put a dollar value on their relationship—less than the price of a haircut.

As we compared our war stories, Keith could hardly take it personal anymore. Our dad *was* who he *was*, no matter which son you happened to be.

As Keith grew into a young man, he had gone to work at a gas station, and for a time, that was enough. It was a respectable job with regular hours and a steady paycheck. And it was more than a lot of young men had at his age. One day a group of his friends drove up in a customized BMW with a girl he liked. They clowned him as he pumped their gas, then threw him a crisp dollar bill and sped off. They had it all, and there stood Keith in grease-stained overalls, hands coated with motor oil and stinking of gasoline.

It was one of those defining scenes in your life where you dearly wish that the one left standing out in the cold isn't you *but it is.*

That was Keith's last day at the station. For the rest of his life, he would be the one in the driver's seat—the cars, the girls, and a career where longevity was rare and tomorrow wasn't written into the contract.

———— • ————

Respect—I finally had it.

Kaos & Mystro's first single and video had dropped. "Mystro on the Flex" was a 1989 hit in Detroit and several midwestern cities and garnered an award for number one video on The Box—a pay-per-view cable network—for the most weeks at the top. A wave of success washed us with admiration, bringing with it opportunities to share stages with Public Enemy, X Clan, EPMD, and many others. As a highly sought-after DJ for big parties, events, and producing, I charged top dollar and got it.

In 1990 the Detroit Pistons won their second NBA title—two years in a row. The air was electric, and my boys and I had decided to ride downtown, where the entire city would join in the celebration. With the top down on the Amigo, we rolled through the streets on our way to a friend's record shop that was on the way. (We'll call this friend Cliff.)

Music blasted from inside as I stood pounding on the door. In the days of pocket change and pay phones, I hustled across the street hoping a telephone call would get his attention. It rang a few times before Cliff answered.

"Hey, open the door!" I yelled, just as a car pulled up beside us.

A group of guys jumped out, aiming guns at us.

"Stay in the phone booth!" one of them yelled at me. "The rest of you, get out of the truck!"

My boys calmly slid out, and they jacked my ride just as Cliff opened the door to the record store.

"What the … " Cliff called out.

"[Expletive] took my truck!" I shouted.

But as the thief behind the wheel hit the gas and one of his boys jumped in, the truck lurched, then slowly picked up speed. Apparently, a talent for pointing guns doesn't make you an expert with a stick shift. The smell of gears grinding permeated the air as Cliff handed me a sawed-off shotgun.

By the time I could get behind them to get a good shot, they were too far to hit with buckshot. I wanted to let one off to release my frustration, but I remembered the many lessons Keith had taught me about being stealthy in retaliation. Retribution would have to wait—but not for very long.

My boys and I raced back to my house to get strapped. By the age of twenty, I was back into martial arts—judo—but I had also acquired a few illegal weapons, my favorite being a .380 semiautomatic that was easier to hide. My mother was frantic, pleading with me not to go after them. I assured her that I was only going to file a police report, but she knew me better than that. Even her frisk at the door as I was leaving came up empty, as Keith had taught me how to break down the gun to avoid detection.

We roamed the city, but after hours of searching, their car and my truck had disappeared. I couldn't believe my truck was gone— one of only two like it in the city—with chrome rims, trim, and sounds. Now I had nothing.

Well, not *nothing* … I had my rep, my boys, and my beats. But a young man without wheels is like a bird without wings. Even perched on the highest peak, he can only look down and dream of soaring on the thermal breeze. Without his impressive wingspan and flamboyant feathers, there's very little difference between a regal eagle and a sitting duck.

Beyond repair.

That was the condition of my truck when the police eventually found it—dismembered and too damaged to save. My wings had been clipped. My first ride, bought for me by my beloved brother, a car now bound to infamy. And Keith was not happy about it. In his eyes, it was nearly unforgivable to be caught off guard without a gun. Suddenly I was back to driving my mother's car.

Where did I think I was going? How many turns of fortune would my life require before it all finally came off the rails? Only Yah knows the day, time, and place of our birth and demise. Yet in Him we can be born all over again after "self" is put to death. Beauty from the ashes.

But my ashes were still in the fire.

10

MY WAY OR
HIS WILL

A person often meets his destiny on the road he took to avoid it.

Jean de La Fontaine, "The Horoscope"

On the night of my twenty-first birthday, the basement—my haven where I kept every piece of music equipment—had flooded, or so Mama warned me as I came through the front door. Sprinting down the stairs, I braced myself for something too awful to imagine.

Only to hear "Surprise!" shouted out by a small army of my closest friends.

It was enough to stop my heart, then restart it again. My mother had coordinated the whole thing. Along with the food, music, and dancing, the owner of the record label I was signed to brought a prerelease copy of the album I produced—another first.

As we all listened, a swell of pride and a rush of legal adulthood told me that I never wanted the evening to end.

It was late, and the crowd was thinning when Nate and I heard about another party being held downtown. He and I drove through Midtown Detroit, stretching a night that comes only once in a young man's life. I was of age—a *man*.

The place was packed by the time we arrived, and they had stopped letting people in. With any luck, one of my boys would be handling security. As I pressed through the impatient crowd waiting outside, I caught the attention of the police. Suddenly an officer's confrontational words were broadcast loud enough for everyone to hear.

"Get the [expletive] away from the door and walk across the street!"

Yes, he was talking to me.

With several members of my family in law enforcement, I knew the respect they deserved. But even as I complied with his demand, apparently I wasn't moving fast enough. Aggressively, he grabbed me and tried to throw me against his squad car. I say, *tried*.

Before I could stop it, my martial art reflexes engaged. Instead of resisting him, I went with his momentum, sidestepped him, and he landed face-first on the hood of his car. *Why couldn't I have pulled that off in the tenth grade?*

You can guess what happened next. I was slammed against the car, handcuffed, and put in the back seat of a squad car. Nate approached and even opened the door to make sure I was okay.

"Oh, you want to go to jail too?" the cop pseudo-asked him before slapping cuffs on Nate and throwing him into the car with me. What added to our confrontation was that the cop was black.

"I couldn't let you go down alone." Nate chuckled.

We had a good laugh all the way to the jail. It seemed funny at the time, but it wasn't. Not really. My twenty-first birthday ended with a night in a cell. My mother bailed me out the next morning, and the ticket was thrown out of court. Thinking back, I can only feel thankful that the year was 1991 instead of 2011. Black men are shot by police for much less these days, leaving their surviving loved ones to ask "Why?"

Why are emotions such a surprise? It's as if they're someone we've never met—a person we've heard about but haven't been introduced to. Then when they emerge in fighting spirit, we're unable to identify them, much less control them. It's a lot like Yah. You may know who He is and things He's said and done. But if you've never personally met Him, talked to Him, and heard His voice, He's a stranger. Unpredictable. At times terrifying. It only makes sense that He chooses to take up residence deep within us, in our hearts. Our emotional home. A place we as men tend to avoid.

———— • ————

Her name was Nicole.

Beyond her physical beauty—yes, I was awestruck—she was an identical twin. My friend Chris knew them from the University of

Michigan and introduced us as we were out shopping for furniture. As I said hello to Natalie, Nicole spoke up.

"Hey, you look familiar. I know you from somewhere," she said as she took a good look at me.

With an ego used to recognition, I smiled confidently. "Yeah, probably Kaos & Mystro. I'm Mystro."

Nicole, on the other hand, wasn't smiling. Not one little bit. "No, that's not it."

I admit that crushed my ego! After a few painful seconds of silence, I glanced over at Chris, who was enjoying the awkward pause between us. Somehow I still walked away with Nicole's phone number and a refurbished sense of self.

A bet is a bet, even when the odds are stacked against you.

Chris deemed it impossible that I could entice a kiss from Nicole before August. He knew that she and her sister were extremely particular when it came to the men they associated with. I'm happy to report that Chris lost that bet, but it wasn't easy. Nicole was in no rush to date because of a turbulent relationship she had prior to meeting me. And let's face it—her daddy was a preacher, and I wasn't known citywide for my "church boy" reputation.

It would take three more months for us to speak about the celebration of Kelly's life—our mutual friend we had lost to a gunshot. It's amazing to think that Nicole was the young girl seated only a few feet from me at Kelly's funeral. She had also been at an Ann Arbor party I deejayed, though I didn't know it at the time. And she was there now as I felt a spiritual awakening beginning in me.

We stood at the epicenter of Yah's calling. From our youth to adulthood, from past to present. Still standing near, just unaware of the future we would be called to—together.

The Most High holds us within the palm of His hand. All of us simultaneously. He weaves our souls so closely within the same tapestry that we're unable to even recognize our future spouses. Time is His servant and our grace. There is never too much or too little of it. And it is Yah that has the final say as time runs out. Even then, we'll be together. Those who are in Him cannot be separated from Him. Time is always on our side.

Typically, I would have ended "the chase" after Nicole's refusal to return my calls. But for reasons beyond explanation, I continued to pursue her, traversing the emotional minefields that accompany the insecurity of a young man's ego and eccentricities. Perhaps even then, the spirit in me understood the spirit in her.

Thanks to Yah (and persuasive words from Natalie), Nicole did give the relationship a chance, although reluctantly. As we moved forward at a snail's pace, I can say without a doubt that it was not the thrill of the chase that kept me interested but my sincere feelings for her. As for Nicole, the roses that I meant as a grand gesture didn't impress her. Truth was, she had more depth than other women tantalized by perfumed flowers and sparkly things. It was simple, genuine acts of kindness that eventually unlocked her heart.

Some men call it soft, sentimental stuff. I call it being real.

Slim in stature, Nicole expressed her interest in gaining a few pounds. And with my experience in weight training, she was happy to accept my help with a meal plan. Yes, it was a small and easy gift to give, but that seemingly insignificant effort would be enough to secure our first date. It's the uncomplicated offerings—those relaxed, unforced encounters—that have built the strongest structures in human relationships and fortified marital commitments the world over.

Deny it all you want, brothers, but home *is* where the heart is.

Finding a new gear—a speed far below the usual limit set for racetracks in my circle—was necessary in order to show my respect for Nicole. She had to feel free to move at her own pace. While out on our first date, though I was dying to put my arm around her, I resisted. Soon enough, she placed her arm around me, which gave me the signal to do the same. The feeling was different, unlike any other dates before it.

We rode around after the movie, talking about all kinds of things—things you wouldn't have the first inclination to discuss under the covers. The walk to her parents' doorstep was also free of incident—no assumptions, no kiss. Waiting patiently for Nicole's trust was far more important to me.

She was a treasure well worth the wait.

Soon my priorities shifted from hangin' with my boys to giving my full attention to Nicole. In the culture of hip-hop, where mantras like "Bros over hos" and "Money over bit" were the law, a young man was considered a "busta" if he violated either one. And it wasn't uncommon to get a beatdown for holding hands with a girl in public. But I was no longer phased by street silliness—for the first time in my life, I allowed the desires of my heart to lead me.

I wanted to settle down, and no one could deny me that.

———— • ————

Can you hear the years pass, song by song? That running soundtrack that overlaps our lives. Music that plays parallel to everything that happens to you. Feelings, memories, emotions. And you can play it back—one year, ten years, twenty years later—and know exactly where you were the instant "it" happened.

On this night, the song would play a near-fatal beat and hook ... hauntingly familiar.

A friend had given me the keys to his truck, and it took only a couple of hours to finish recording the track at the studio before heading back to the brownstone. It was about 11:00 p.m. and the highway was clear. He needed the beats in order to write over them, and I had the sound blasting as my head bobbed to the beats I had just made.

There's something very freeing about driving alone, especially in a nice ride. All was well with the world, and it was one of those rare nights when you exhale and let down your guard. But Detroit is the last city you should drop your guard in. As we used to say, "chillin' like a villain." In other words, stay alert.

Up ahead but out of sight, a car had stalled in my lane. There were no hazard lights, no signs of anything. Just low beams and thirty feet of visibility. Fast, free, and clear. By the time I saw the car motionless in front of me, it was too late. The soundtrack kept going.... Typically I would create hip-hop tracks between eighty-five and ninety-five beats per minute, but this rhythm felt like three beats per second!

First beat ...

I pulled the wheel and the truck swerved. The wheels locked as I hit the brakes. A sickening feeling of helplessness and dread brought deadly silence as if sound was too much distraction. So Yah pressed "mute."

Second beat ...

The truck collided with the median and went airborne, flipping twice. I had a surreal view of the world through the windshield, tipping end over end. I braced for impact.

Third beat ...

Like a juggernaut, the truck crashed to the ground with metal bending, glass shattering, and its passenger still breathing. The soundtrack came back ... accelerating to the speed of life.

I heard the high-pitched squeal of an ambulance siren that was faint at first but gradually got louder. The world was right side up again, and I was on my back on an EMT's stretcher.

In the emergency room, all I could think about was the truck and the condition it must be in. Even though I made it out with only minor injuries—shaken and bruised—my friend ran in, crying as if I had lost a limb.

"Dawg, you got to get yourself together!" he pleaded.

"What you mean?" I said. "I'm straight. They just got me on the stretcher for precaution. Don't trip."

"No," he said, "my mother told me this was going to happen!"

My friend's mom, a religious woman, had urged her son earlier (after getting a vision) not to drive or ride in the truck. She warned him that someone would have an accident in it. As fate would have it, that someone was me.

Then I remembered all the times I had stared up at the name of Jesus in glowing stars on Sinclair's ceiling. Instantly I knew *who* it was speaking to me. I recognized Him.

I should have died that night … on the third beat. But Yah was in charge of the music.

Was the crash an accident or a message? The Voice that whispered the way to a higher purpose, the miracle of what had just happened, I simply let slip away.

Even though he brought a longtime friend and pastor to speak with me, my friend's company and conversation weren't enough to persuade me. I still believed that the "Jesus mythology" was a misguided message and utterly irrelevant to me.

And the beat went on.

11

NO OTHER GODS

"You must not make for yourself an idol of any kind....
I, the LORD *your God, am a jealous God who will*
not tolerate your affection for any other gods."

Exodus 20:4–5

Every man has an idol.

Whether it's Luke Skywalker or Darth Vader, Batman or the Joker, Black Panther or Killmonger, he will choose the one that has the best chance of saving the day or saving *him.* But unlike fictional characters who wear their identities so distinctly—like a comic book logo on the cover of their deeds—a human being brings both good and evil together under one unified but conflicted seal.

A kindhearted killer, a sentimental rapist, an honorable drug dealer. These polarized features in people can make a contemptible character. That is, if you don't happen to know them, be related to them, *love* them. Most of us put our faith in the underdog, and isn't that what we all want to be? To win against all odds, to redeem our mistakes, to prove that we're not as weak as we appear to be.

I think the vast majority of us wrestle relentlessly, fearful that if we live by the light within us, it will expose the darkness in us to those around us. Insecurities, self-hate, unresolved anger.

That's when I noticed it. I was starting to lose hope. I could feel it leaving day by day, week by week. The vision I had focused on for so long was fading. The dream was slipping away.

Plan B is never as good …

But it's something.

If it turned out that a music career wasn't in my future, I could always fall back on hustling for my idol—my brother Keith. There was a lot to admire about the lifestyle—the money, power, women. My brother wore ten-carat diamond rings, and $100K Piguet watches, drove expensive cars, owned businesses—you name it. Danger surrounded him, and still somehow he made it look good.

He once said, "Jason, if I turn up missing, don't bother to come for me. I'm already dead."

That's why involving me in selling drugs wasn't an option. He always believed I could do better, and he wasn't willing to jeopardize the life of his brother. Only himself.

Gone were the days of deejaying, fallen by the wayside to leave room for producing opportunities. However, Keith continued to encourage me by gifting a coveted Akai MPC60-II sampling drum machine. Spending hours together, listening to stories, I realized our father had left the same disturbing imprint on him, which gave me fresh insight. Another broken young man disregarded and abandoned. I felt for him—for the empty part that still needed filling. And my presence was a reminder of all that pain.

It had been a long time since he had seen Dad.

I couldn't help but wonder—was I the tie that connected them? Then, out of the blue, Keith phoned me to say he was ready to reconcile with our father. But how that reunion would play out, I wasn't sure. Still, I arranged for them to meet after hours at the barbershop where Dad worked.

Keith brought an olive branch—a very expensive olive branch.

An occasion as important as this one needed a peace offering. And what better prize than a two-tone Rolex with a diamond bezel to express his love? Keith lifted up the relationship to where he hoped it could stay. The time for reclamation was at hand. I wasn't there, but I tried to imagine my dad's reaction to such an extravagant gift. What do you say to that kind of generosity?

Regardless, Keith said that finally connecting with him was worth the effort. It seemed, for a while, that rebuilding the bridge between two lands was a daring yet doable venture. But could such a fragile structure find solid ground waiting for it on each side, or would the whole thing come tumbling down?

Later that year, Keith gave Dad one last gift. A large sum of money, enough for him to buy a building to finally open his own barbershop. But when Dad spent it on "other things," he wounded Keith beyond repair. In true Oliver fashion, he thoughtlessly dismissed Keith's emotions, and they never spoke again.

In Keith's zeal to prove that he was grown, successful, and worth a father's pride, he missed something—Oliver's own inability to make that extraordinary leap. It took more energy than he was willing to give. He was hopelessly caught up in his own pride. Our father's universe had only one center, and it was him.

Even someone carrying a golden olive branch can burn up when flying too close to the sun.

———— • ————

The price a boxer pays to take a hit can make life an expensive proposition, both physically and financially. Some find that the high cost can eventually make it not worth living.

Keith and I were traveling everywhere, but Las Vegas kept calling us back as Keith became more heavily involved in promoting the sport of boxing. He even contemplated letting me fight for his team, but to him, the price was too high to send his own little brother into the ring, no matter how hard I could hit.

Soon he was promoting Tom "Boom Boom" Johnson, who was a Detroit transplant fighting his way up the ranks. Initially told he would never make it as a pro, Boom proved himself once and for all on February 26, 1993, when he won the IBF featherweight championship during a rematch with Manuel Medina. He would go on to successfully defend the title eleven times. When he won that fight, Keith was ecstatic—for Boom Boom and for himself, for helping to promote such an incredible match.

And as fortune would have it, it was about nine months later that a music production deal with a company out of Atlanta looked imminent. The dream was on its way back to me.

I immediately called Keith to tell him the good news, and he shared my happiness. He was my go-to. My rock. The person I could trust for an encouraging word, male reassurance, and inspiration to reach higher. It was all lining up—a beautiful girlfriend, a promising future, and a brother to cheer me on.

Life felt almost whole.

———— • ————

The Bowe versus Holyfield match dubbed "Repeat or Revenge" was televised from Caesars Palace on November 6, 1993, and Nicole and I decided to watch the fight at Gabe's house. It was packed and charged with excitement, but my mind was on Keith.

I was the last person to talk to him in the early afternoon days before. His fiancée and I knew that it wasn't like Keith to not come home after a night out. We searched for days and even checked the city morgue. Thank Yah he wasn't there.

Word was that he was last seen in a black van, so every dark-colored vehicle on the road caught my eye as I drove all over town. Still nothing. All the while, his words echoed in my mind: "If I turn up missing …"

When Holyfield came on strong to take rounds 4, 5, and 6 (eventually winning the fight), Gabe started surfing channels. A spattering of commercials flew across the screen along with prime-time shows and a random news update. The report told of the body of a man found in an abandoned van on the east side.

"That's Keith!" I yelled, then fell to my knees, crying inconsolably.

Keith had been kidnapped, tortured, and murdered.

I couldn't believe what I was hearing, what I was feeling. I had just spoken to him. I could still hear his voice in my ears and see him sitting behind the wheel of his truck, doing business on his phone. One more brother of mine, dead. Someone's idol; someone's enemy. Or was he an everyday man who wrestled endlessly, fearful that his dark side would eventually overtake his light?

It was in a drugstore parking lot that I met a piece of myself wearing diamond rings, rising on golden wings, dreaming of so many things.

Is it possible to idolize a man who has everything to lose and winds up with nothing to give? Does it really make a difference in the end?

———— • ————

Looking at Keith lying quietly, asleep eternally, I thought how useless the cushions of a casket were. How they did little to comfort those they were meant to pacify—aching people peering into the face of one so young, so still. After a minute or two, I took a seat next to Gabe. My mother was one of the last people to walk past the casket before it was closed. Within seconds, Mama burst into tears, crying so hard I heard attendees in the row in front of me whisper, "That must be his mother."

Like at Larry's funeral, the church was standing room only with the majority of people in their twenties. And one vacant seat for my dad. Apparently, Keith's death was more than his conscience could stand. I was incensed that he would find his conscience now—some mislaid guilt that happened to appear the same time as his son's obituary. I guess he hadn't forgotten how he treated Keith the last year of his life, but it was too late to make amends. So he stayed away until it was time for the recessional.

"We don't know where Keith is going, but do you know where you're going?" the pastor boldly asked.

He was a stereotypical black Baptist pastor—Jheri curl and a three-piece suit—but he knew how to preach the truth to the lost. No pimping, no heavy breathing, no hollering, just power! It was easy to respect a man like that, and his conviction and intensity had to be admired.

A steady stream of cars snaked its way to the cemetery where Keith's body was laid to rest. Always at the crossroads, he seemed to search for an escape—a way out of "the game"—but never found it. I wondered if I had accepted Christ's call at the age of twenty, maybe I could have prevented Keith's fall.

The personalized plate on one of his drag-racing cars had the inscription *If It's God's Will, I Will.*

I once asked him, "Why do you have that plate on your car when it seems like His will doesn't matter?"

Almost repentantly, he answered, "All I can do is try."

Rest in peace, my dear brother. Rest in peace.

———— • ————

Life comes in and life goes out, like the seasons changing or the ocean's tide as it ebbs and flows. The following year, I was in Chicago on a producing job when I got the call from Nicole.

"You're going to be a father!"

Say what?

A brand-new life was coming straight for me. I was going to be a dad! As first-time parents, our combined excitement, anxieties, and hectic schedules filled our days. Nicole was in her junior year of college, and I was still pursuing music.

The thought of raising a child had me seriously reevaluating everything I was doing. A person sharing my genetic code was about to enter the world, and this took planning and provision. This was my child, my family, and I alone was responsible for his or her future. And as much as this birth challenged my current lifestyle, I put away my drum machine to search for a reliable job.

Thanks to a longtime friend, two weeks before my child was born, I began working on the loading dock of the Detroit Coca-Cola plant. It was a far cry from the glitz of the music industry with singles dropping and videos feeding the producer in me. And I'll say it up front—I hated it! Shifts from 2:30 p.m. to 2:30 a.m., working twelve-hour days, sometimes seven days a week. It was brutal—humid, sweaty, and tiring.

Was this what family life looked like up close? I'd seen other parents sacrifice themselves—deny their desires in order to provide for the family. I had seen how to be the *wrong* kind of father. Now it was my turn to be the right kind.

My supervisor was a slave driver and the first black man I'd witnessed with a bizarre animosity toward his own race. There's nothing like punching the clock of a demanding job only to find yourself on the receiving end of demeaning treatment and disparaging comments. I may have become accustomed to hearing them from my father, but to tolerate rude and disrespectful behavior from other men inflamed the anger that still bubbled just below the surface.

"Hey, guys, your checks won't be here until tomorrow," he taunted one day. "I don't feel sorry for y'all"—referring to the black men present—"but I sure do feel sorry for the white boys who work *really* hard."

It took everything in me not to throw my Coke can at him. But for all I knew, that kind of contempt was established long ago with the infamous letter by Willie Lynch. The slave master's manual emphasized that the best way to keep black people under control was to subliminally teach them how to hate one another. It worked and sadly is still working today.

But on the morning our beautiful daughter, Alexis, was born, any residual anger I had was diluted by a love I had never known. Nothing could have prepared me for that feeling. What preoccupies your every waking thought with one little soul? What convinces you to work a job you can't stand, gets you up at all hours, and folds you in half at a gurgle or grin?

It was an experience unlike any I'd had before.

Alexis was the first grandbaby on both sides, so she never wanted for attention. Everyone vied to hold her, feed her, play with her. Mama especially, always having dreamed of a daughter.

The first time I held her in my arms and looked at that tiny face, I was infatuated. This was when my life transformed from being all about me to committing everything I had to those beautiful brown eyes.

My heart was now beating for three: my daughter, Nicole, and me.

———— • ————

Sacrifice was a word taking on new meaning as I worked tirelessly to ensure the health and happiness of my new family. Calling Nicole during my daily lunch break gave me a sense of joy that existed only outside Coke's factory walls, encouraging me to endure another shift. Although one day I found myself venting. It may have started out about work, but it ended up as a heated exchange about the God she put so much trust in. Nicole knew that I believed in Him and that He was calling me. But actively seeking Him wasn't on my calendar. I despised church! And if I denied Yah's presence, maybe that Voice inside me would go away.

"God isn't real. If He was, then why am I working like a slave when I'm gifted at doing something else?"

After devoting years to music, I couldn't figure out how the Most High could leave me in such a difficult place without any obvious way of escape. The thought of a God supposedly so rich in mercy was difficult, but the idea of Yahushua being my personal Savior was even more offensive.

We debated, argued, and routinely disagreed. My stance on the subject never varied: no way would I accept the idea of God's Son coming from the sky—through the clouds—to show up to save us. I put more faith in the Egyptology material I was reading and referred to Ra (the sun god) as the only "sun" coming through the clouds. Nicole tried to calm me while staying firm, which aggravated me more. Her blind faith in someone I was convinced wasn't there only made things worse.

In frustration, I said, "God isn't real!" then hung up.

Ten minutes later, a shipment of pallets had arrived just as they did every night. As I climbed into my Hi-Lo forklift and moved toward the loading dock, the Most High had His sights on me. As I drove onto the truck, the weight of the Hi-Lo pushed the truck bed away, separating it from the dock.

The driver had failed to lock the brakes.

No matter who argues *what* in this world, scientists all agree— ain't nothing you can do about gravity.

I began falling …

I didn't see it coming, couldn't stop it from happening, had no time to reconsider my religious convictions or deny Nicole's beloved Jesus.

Just falling. A descent a decade in the making.

I traveled eight feet before hitting the ground, landing with a shudder on my side mere feet from the overturned forklift. With the force hard enough to herniate two disks in my back, I couldn't move. The pain was excruciating, and the shock of plummeting dazed me.

But I was still breathing.

And as quickly as the Hi-Lo had fallen, the truck began rolling backward toward me. I braced for impact as that 18-wheeler closed the gap. In that blink of an eye, I thought about the conversation Nicole and I just had and all those years I ran from Yah's calling.

In agony, I could do nothing but watch as the Hi-Lo's forks slowly slid downward, stopping the truck's momentum just before it struck the forklift, tipping it over on me.

A mere ten minutes after arguing about whether God was there, I knew. He was there, and He *did* care.

This was no accident but a summons, an immediate response to my resistance to Yah's calling on my life. And as I lay there gazing up at the stars, they seemed so familiar, like the glow-in-the-dark stars on Sinclair's bedroom ceiling. Was *Jesus* written in the sky that night, and was He coming back for me whether I was ready or not? I shed tears at the sight and for the Son who was on my side.

"I'll never go against You again," I promised. "Never again."

No other idols. No other gods. Only You, Yah … only You.

12

UNCOMPROMISED CONVICTION

Lead strong. Once you've compromised, you're no longer leading.

Jimmie D. Compton Jr.

I had a wedding to attend in the morning—my wedding!

It was a sultry July evening at the church when I kissed Nicole as we finished the rehearsal. Our three-year-old daughter, Alexis, had practiced her part of quintessential flower girl, scattering petals from a basket that dwarfed her. This wasn't Nicole's ideal marriage scenario— one that included her own child—but it was a sweet blessing that would only enhance the day's atmosphere with giggles and smiles.

As Nicole's father was senior pastor, he would preside over the ceremony in front of a multitude of friends and family.

My relationship with Pastor Smith started out rocky. Nicole's dad was protective, and rightly so. The bickering between Nicole and me before Alexis was born was rooted in immaturity and didn't go unnoticed by him or others. But as I took ownership of my childishness and overcame much of it, Pastor Smith and I found common ground in our mutual love for Nicole.

My hours at work were long and grueling and would often finish at 2:30 in the morning. But with Nicole and Alexis still living under his roof, Pastor Smith always left his door open to me. Nothing was more important to him than family. He was a man of understanding, stable and supportive. Exactly what a father should be—the kind of father I wanted to be.

Mrs. Smith and I got along instantly, and our lively debates about Christ revealed a lot about her. In those days, I complained that time pointlessly spent in church was irretrievable—lost forever—like a wallet you accidentally leave on the subway. Without raising her voice or showing condemnation of any kind, she would say, "Jason, I can't argue about what God did for me. But I pray He will reveal Himself to you."

Prayer is a mighty thing, especially when it's your future mother-in-law doing the praying! From her lips to Yah's ears, those prayers were heard, received, and answered. Much like my brother Sinclair, she had unlimited access to the throne and took full advantage of it.

How does Yah do it—take a devastating accident that could have left me crippled and stuck physically, mentally, and spiritually and turn it into the very thing that liberated me? An accident that drove me from intolerant irreverence to divine reconciliation within an eight-foot drop. Now I was about to walk down the aisle toward a brand-new life with the woman I loved, a daughter I adored, and a Friend with the power of the universe at His command.

It seemed that the worst was behind me.

I kissed Nicole again as the church rehearsal ended, and we all headed over to my mother's house for a crowded rehearsal dinner.

———— • ————

Still in pain, my back injury kept me from returning to work. It also justified bringing a lawsuit against the trucking company whose driver was at fault. Now, with limited mobility (for the time being), how would I provide for Nicole, Alexis, and myself? I could think of only one thing that made any sense at all.

A first love is never lost.

In the past, music had been my strength, and it still was—deep inside me, exactly where I had left it.

Back in the studio, I was growing, absorbing and applying all the lessons that accumulate with every personality that makes a contribution to your skill set. But as with most education, no matter what the topic or how it translates to life, there comes a learning curve where we feel the bend of the metal, the uncomfortable twist of the mold, until it fits the revised *us*.

Have you ever wondered why "new wine" never goes into "old wineskins" (Matt. 9:17)? It was a Scripture I would learn the meaning of firsthand.

Faith—my faith—was undeniable to everyone around me. And when my commitment to that faith was challenged, it was made all the more real. I had stopped drinking and cursing; I had nailed my old self to the cross, which drew me into a deeper dialogue with Yah about the direction I was going. But great strides are sometimes met with equal resistance, and newfound philosophies will be subject to probing questions. Some you'll be able to answer, and some you won't.

Like me, you'll have two choices: move forward or go backward, advance or retreat. There is no middle ground when serving Yah; you are either with Him or against Him.

Zealous in reaching out to those who were still stumbling in the darkness, I felt the irresistible urge and obligation to guide them into the light. If I could illuminate the path ahead for just one person, that would be one fewer soul wandering in the wilderness. A wilderness I was well acquainted with—still.

But it was my unwillingness to get off the fence that was compromising my own walk, staying safely neutral within the nonbelieving status quo of my worldly friends. That's no way to represent Someone who's taken a bullet for you. However, if your heart remains pure and stayed on Him, Yah will help you make the choice. Bend your metal—your *normal,* sometimes to the breaking point—to ease you into the indestructible mold designed especially for your "new man."

Still, our free will can make that choice difficult, and you can bet that although Yah wishes none would perish, He will never interfere with it.

———— • ————

From hip-hop to Egyptology to Christianity, the conversation developed like storm clouds in the distance with the kind of rain you can smell before a drop falls, knowing any minute a torrential downpour could soak you right through to your bone-dry inflexibility.

We leaned against the kitchen table as our personal views on each subject brought faint sounds of thunder. Not anger, just a slight rumble of opinion as a rapper listened to me proclaim my faith with conviction about the relationship I had with Christ. It was a compelling testimony, or so I thought, until his manager came in and voiced his own opinion—one equivalent to a lightning strike.

"Don't listen to him! How can he be a Christian when he just produced the song where you guys are talkin' about gettin' high and sleeping with host?"

A direct hit!

They left the room, laughing, as Yahushua gently spoke to me through an echo of Scripture. "No one can serve two masters" (Matt. 6:24).

I couldn't stand hypocrites, especially in the church. To me, there were few things worse. And there I was, straddling the line, suddenly feeling nauseated. In my effort to reach the lost, I had become what I despised. And like the gracious yet faithful Lord He is, Yah rained on my pious parade so that I might rise to the clear blue faith above. Without compromise or mediocrity, my forward motion was finally lining up with my faith.

A change was imminent. It was time to get off the fence!

Gone from my music were the lyrics that promoted violence, drugs, sex, and murder. Everything I attached my name to moving forward had to glorify the Most High. And though I would no longer produce music for secular artists, our personal relationships endured. My nonconformity to the world had made an impression—one they respected.

Yah's fingerprints were beginning to appear everywhere.

I was speaking His language. Discerning His wishes. Following in His narrow path. I was finding peace where there once was pandemonium. I was in the world but steadily taking myself out of it. I was an alien, a foreigner passing through. And within that journey of discovery, Yah sent people to teach and guide me.

It's amazing how the Most High introduces us to individuals at the most appropriate moments. His all-knowing perspective allows Him to address our needs before we're even aware we have them and aligns people with what He's doing in us.

That was the summer I met Shannon Gaston. We were the same age, and he was the first Christian brother to befriend me after I surrendered my life to Christ. Our souls spontaneously connected, as we were both heavy into Egyptology before our conversions. He also loved hip-hop, which bound us tighter still.

But the most profound quality about Shannon was his ability to "walk out" his Christian beliefs without compromise. He lived what he preached, which taught me more than even our shared Bible studies. He was a walking, talking expression of Christ's guidance through example. I now had a growing group of exemplary men in my life proving that it was possible to live with conviction without compromising. Like Shannon, instead of looking for validation in temporary things, I was investing in the eternal.

I had found my new identity.

———— • ————

When the court settlement with the trucking company was finalized, there was enough money for Nicole and me to close on our first house a week before the wedding. Another loving nod from Yah. The house was small, but it was ours. It wasn't Nicole's initial choice, but I promised that after the renovations I was prepared to do, it would be a place she would love coming home to.

But for now, there was a wedding in the works!

As my groomsmen drove us down the main street from the church rehearsal toward my mother's house, I could still see Nicole and Alexis in our car through the spotty traffic. The entire wedding party was on its way to meet for the rehearsal dinner.

But my boys had other plans ...

With the ceremony looming large the next day, my friends took it on themselves to secretly orchestrate the ultimate bachelor party. And as typical "night before the wedding" protocol would have it, I went along, though reluctant and uneasy. We soon pulled into the undisclosed location.

All Stars was known for the best-looking girls in the city and being one of the hottest strip clubs in Detroit. Looking up at the sign, I felt an instant rush of adrenaline mixed with guilt.

Loyalty—it's a slippery slope.

Not wanting to offend them by refusing, I couldn't take the risk of coming off holier than thou. Amid the heat of naked bodies, we found a table, and within minutes, my friends had ordered me a lap dance. But instead of being aroused by the usual male impulses, I was disgusted. The old Jason had been replaced by the new one—the one taking the road less traveled.

I kept it cool, looking unaffected by it all. I wanted to enjoy the company of my friends on a night out. But as time wore on, my spirit became increasingly troubled. I finally told them to meet me outside when they were ready to leave.

From a pristine church sanctuary to the dirty parking lot of a Shake Shack—this was not where I had pictured myself on the eve of my wedding.

Another twenty or thirty minutes and they all piled out of the club in the best of moods. As we drove to my mother's house, I was indignant at the cheap sexual display that felt inappropriate for a grown man of the Most High, especially hours before the most important day of his life.

My wedding rehearsal dinner was taking place! At least, it *had* taken place.

As we arrived, Nicole and her bridesmaids were getting ready to leave. In fact, the entire wedding dinner was over. The atmosphere was tense; everyone felt it. My mother stared at me with *that look*, but that was nothing compared with the words I got from my future wife.

Nicole was more angry than hurt. As we stood on the porch saying our good-byes, she knocked the wind out of me with a painful truth.

"Mr. Minister, at the strip club … what would your friends say about that?" She didn't say it in a condemning way but in a "Holy Spirit, you deal with him" kind of way.

I had no words—not one that could excuse or explain my behavior.

Then she added, "I didn't know I was marrying a hypocrite."

Another lightning strike, splitting wide my integrity, leaving it smoldering.

Nicole was well aware of how sold out to Christ I was and that inside, I was good. She also knew that I'd had no desire to go to the club that night. But I couldn't blame her for her reaction. I was to blame. It was my decision to go along with the crowd and let others dictate my actions. And now I had to accept the consequences.

I stood in front of my mother's house, angry, with tears in my eyes as Nicole drove away. All I wanted was for her to trust me with her future, with our child, and to make her happy. Look what I had done.

Hypocrite. The very word Christ used to confront the religious leaders of His day (see Matt. 23). That was not me! It couldn't be me.

Inside my mother's house, my church's youth pastor, Dennis Talbert, could see how upset I was. He called me into the back room along with our brother in Christ, Shannon.

"Don't let the Devil take from you what God intends for you to learn from this," Pastor Talbert told me.

In the minutes that followed, the three of us prayed, and my emotions settled as Yah spoke to my spirit.

Soon my groomsmen huddled with me, confused by the seriousness of the situation. They just didn't get it. And why should they?

"What's wrong, Jay?" they said, mystified by my misery.

Before I could speak, tears began streaming down my face. I thought, *Yo, what's going on! I can't cry in front of my boys! This is weak!*

"I'm not the guy I used to be," I finally stated, as if announcing a death.

"Yo, Jay, it's all good! We just wanted you to have fun the night before you got married. Our fault!"

"No, you don't understand. It's not your fault; it's mine. I should have been more outspoken with my faith. If I had been, you wouldn't have taken me there! I need you to know now that I'm not doing the things I used to do. Those days are over."

There it was. I had run the gauntlet, set the bar, and now they knew. And as quickly as I said the words, I felt relieved. I would never again give them a reason to question my morality. And I could see in their eyes I still had their respect.

With my mind and heart on Nicole, I stayed awake into the small hours of the night, writing lyrics for a surprise song that my friend Maurice would sing at the wedding. It was my job to reassure her that she was marrying not a hypocrite but a redeemed man of the Most High.

———— • ————

This is really happening.

When morning came, I was still troubled by the way I had disappointed Nicole. I gathered with my groomsmen as we gave one another dap and cracked jokes to ease the tension. We took our positions near the altar as soft music began to play. And just as I convinced myself that the onslaught of emotions would not get the better of me, someone walked in.

It was my dad.

He looked so weak and fragile with barely enough strength to make it to the front row, where he finally sat down, winded and struggling. His wife, Betty, was by his side.

My father had developed Parkinson's disease. He was still strong mentally, but physically it was starting to get the best of him. I had been told that he was beginning to suffer and that there was a good chance he wouldn't make it to the wedding. After cutting his clientele in half and working from a sitting position, he lacked the stamina to continue at his normal pace at the barbershop.

Now, with the life draining out of him, he couldn't run away from me anymore. An ironic twist of fate—he spent what little strength was left to make it back to me. All the times he deflected, put down, or ignored me. The abusive words and continuous lack of interest. The love lost within his shortsighted, selfish tunnel vision. But there he was, right in front of me, making up for countless times I needed him.

The last grand gesture to heal twenty-five years of hurt.

I could hardly believe it was all happening.

One by one, beginning with my daughter and her basket of flowers, the wedding party made their way up the aisle. As the wedding march played, lifting up years of wishing, waiting, Nicole appeared. I was awestruck! She was always beautiful, but on that day of days, she was resplendent. In a word: *sacred*. Eagerly taking her hand from her father, I gazed into her eyes. We then faced the altar as her dad took his place as pastor and proceeded with the marriage vows.

I admit now that I lacked a true biblical understanding of what was taking place—to appreciate what the joining of two people truly represented. Marriage is not just a license to spiritually legalize sex but a serious covenant with the Most High God. Yet in the sight of His Holy Spirit, I made light of it, cracking jokes about how the singer reminded me of Sexual Chocolate from *Coming to America*.

They say youth is wasted on the young, and looking back, I tend to agree. If I had it to do over again, I would surely find the reverence for what the Most High was giving me and for the incredible woman who was being placed in my care. Also, for the new beginning that I could have missed entirely.

After the wedding ceremony, we all enjoyed a lavish reception at the Cobo Hall Ballroom located in downtown Detroit. It was an opulent affair in the gorgeous hall with floor-to-ceiling windows that tantalized with a view of Canada. Then my new bride and I headed off on our much-anticipated honeymoon—paradise in the sun. But even paradise has its share of storm clouds.

Yah, please … no more lightning.

13

A RECKLESS PURSUIT OF RESPECT

To be one, to be united is a great thing. But to respect the right to be different is maybe even greater.

Bono

Leaving Detroit for a five-day honeymoon in Jamaica was one of our better ideas.

The first night was, in a word, *memorable*. We had found the perfect spot to unwind and enjoy the beautiful surroundings. The colorful flowers, the sounds of the ocean—it was all so tranquil and calming. Looking out at the sunset each night, you would swear you were in heaven if not for the frequent smell of marijuana, a pungent odor that hung in the air.

But even a blissful tropical fantasy has people in it, which always brings it back down to earth—and not always in a good way. This truth couldn't have been plainer than when we were standing in the buffet line for breakfast one morning. The woman and her husband in front of us were ordering their meal from the resort cook.

Politely the husband asked the chef, "How about eggs and curry chicken?"

The cook looked at him, then at his wife, and replied, "I don't know, but how about I take your wife out and show her what a real man is?"

"Hey, man, just make my food," the husband responded.

And that was it! The exchange ended with the husband walking away with his wife and letting a total stranger disrespect both of them.

On my worst day, I would never let anyone play me like that. Where I was from, a man's raw nerves and emotional trigger finger could get you killed. One diss and your life could end.

Next in line, I mentally prepared myself for the worst-case scenario. I wasn't a thug, but like Tupac said, "I ain't a killer, but don't push me."[1] With muscles flexed, I approached the cook and intensely stared him down while Nicole ordered for us without incident.

While there's nothing wrong with a husband expressing indignation about foolishness, I realized that the "old man" inside me was still in there, but he was now a strange hybrid of unresolved anger restrained by a higher power.

And my emotions were about to be tested again.

———— • ————

They called him Jamaican Elvis! And if he weren't so offensive, I'd be laughing right along with you.

It was the job of Jamaican Elvis to walk around the villas at dusk, playing his guitar for the guests during dinner. Since he was part of our vacation package, our villa was next on his tour of the resort suites. I tried my best to discourage Nicole from allowing him in, but she insisted.

Just go with the flow, Jason, I told myself. *Go with the flow.* I decided to keep the jokes about his cheesy impression to myself.

But no sooner had I made that resolution than I heard him singing as he approached, and I knew I wouldn't like the dude. Call it a sixth sense, subconscious identification, sizing somebody up, or whatever you want. But when I opened the door and he strode in right past me like some kind of gift from above, my mind was made up.

Five feet tall with his shirt unbuttoned, his Rico Suave demeanor forced me to find a new gear for my patience. He started to croon as we continued with our meal, and I couldn't believe how irritated he made me. All I wanted was for him to stop singing and take his Tom Selleck mustache on out the door to his next villa gig. Maybe the husband or boyfriend next on his hit list would appreciate him more than me, but I doubted it.

After about five minutes, he got real comfortable—with Nicole, that is. And suddenly I started feeling like the husband who was disrespected in the breakfast line. It was as if I wasn't there, invisible to this karaoke gigolo. And before I could believe what was happening, he was full-on serenading my wife!

"Bro, it's time for you to go!" I didn't try to filter out the contempt in my voice.

Nicole's mouth dropped. She was completely embarrassed as I escorted that busta out as if I was security. A guitar and a little chest hair and some men think they can take over the world.

Paradise ... I was beginning to rethink that description.

For the most part, we did enjoy the rest and relaxation of our honeymoon. But at the end of those five days, it's safe to say we were both ready to get back to our daughter and new home. So much work needed to be done to the house, but "passion projects" aren't really labor. Just love in action.

———— • ————

That same year, Chris Webber's album 2 *Much Drama* finally released. The single I produced, "Gangsta! Gangsta!" charted *Billboard*'s Top 100 Songs, and Kurupt congratulated me on soon becoming a platinum producer. That's why I was baffled when the album was not promoted. Later, I was told that with its explicit content, the album could have easily cost Chris several of—if not all—his million-dollar endorsement deals. He made the best decision for his NBA career.

However, a manager contacted me to say that he had an upcoming meeting with some of the best rappers in the industry and urged me to send him my demo. In my excitement to get the demo CD to the FedEx outlet, I rushed out of the house, forgetting that my sweet three-year-old daughter was in her room asleep.

I was halfway to FedEx—less than ten minutes away—before I realized that I had left Alexis alone.

I quickly turned around.

As I drove up my street, police cars were already in front of the house. With Nicole at work for the Red Cross, I had set the alarm before leaving, and my baby girl had gotten out of bed and set it off. When the police arrived, she let them in.

I squeezed her tight with tears in my eyes. "I'm sorry. I'm so sorry." What else could I say? What I did was unforgivable.

The lead police officer was more than gracious considering the circumstances but said he had to report the incident to Protective Services. He warned me that I may get a call, but praise Yah, it never came.

That was the last gracious warning from Yah that I needed. My dreams for a career as a music producer ground to a halt, and I no longer sought money for my music. I needed a more stable income to provide for Nicole and Alexis in a way that wouldn't compromise my convictions.

I began a new company called LME Home Enhancement that specialized in ceramic and marble. The initials reflected my music production company, Lord Maji Entertainment—just keepin' the dream close. Having fully recovered from my back injury, within four years I was installing tile in the homes of millionaire business owners and NBA stars. It was hard not to be proud of my accomplishments, and in the seven years of owning and operating LME, I never received a single customer complaint.

While I was building the foundations of homes for Metro Detroit's wealthy, the Most High was building my own spiritual foundation. He and I were finally on the same page.

———— • ————

It was too soon to be fighting … as if *any time* is a good time.

A man makes decisions, and those decisions are his own. I had my reasons for staying at Rosedale Park Baptist Church. After surrendering my life to Yah, I had made it my church home with friends and supporters who lifted me up as I gradually grew in my faith and walk with Christ. My pastors, teachers, and those helping disciple me were more valuable than any platinum album could ever be. Why should I be expected to leave a church I loved just because Nicole's father was a pastor in charge of his own flock?

In 1999 my wife and I—though unified in love—were divided in our home. I had managed to become self-righteous about it all. Nicole was still a member of her father's congregation, and she refused to join the church I was attending, although she would visit Rosedale every now and then. And the fact that her father never stepped in only added fuel to the fire. It was clear to me that Nicole was being unbiblical by not following me to Rosedale. Still, my father-in-law never reinforced this.

And it infuriated me.

I didn't know that he had made a choice—as a father—to not intrude in his daughter's decision-making. And to some extent, he wouldn't even give advice unless asked. As I said, he esteemed family greatly and never wanted to jeopardize his own. I too wanted to be the man of my own home, leading my wife and daughter as I followed Christ.

There's something very special about creating your own unique legacy and family traditions, and that was my motivation (excluding any pride I was dealing with). But as I stayed the course, doing what I thought was right, it put a strain on my marriage and the relationship between me and my in-laws.

Family is irreplaceable, and I cherished mine with every breath. Alexis was Daddy's girl; she was my heartbeat! Wherever I was, she was there, just hanging out for hours as I videotaped much of our playtimes together.

Then something astonishing took place—she started to grow up. It seemed to happen overnight. One day she was a baby giggling and pinching my nose, and the next she had a mind and attitude of her own. And like a reflex I couldn't control, I became over-protective and self-righteous. Instead of loving her unconditionally through her tween years, I criticized seemingly every decision she made and every desire she had that wasn't literally written in the Bible. My actions weren't rooted in love, but I was so heavenly minded that I was no longer any earthly good.

My religious ways caused me to forget that people are drawn to the heavenly Father not through His wrath but through His loving-kindness. I can say the same about human fathers and their children. It's incredibly difficult for a dad to see his child suddenly discovering his or her own view of the world, disregarding the father's sensibilities. Is it out of concern, ego, or personal experience of having traveled the road before him or her? It must be all three. But Yah creates us to be individuals. He lovingly designs us to be set apart.

And Alexis was to be set apart for His glory—a divine reflection of her heavenly Father, not her earthly dad. I repented to Yah for trying to be Alexis's Holy Spirit; I got out of His way so He could gradually grow her into the person He desired. His living, breathing construction site—a structure fit for His Spirit to live in.

A human home to inhabit ...

Like you.

Like me.

NOTE

1. Tupac Shakur, vocalist, "Hail Mary," by Tupac Shakur, Young Noble, and Kastro, released March 7, 1997, single on The Don Killuminati: The 7 Day Theory, Interscope Records, CD.

14

TWO HALVES BECOMING WHOLE

God puts rainbows in the clouds so that each of us—in the dreariest and most dreaded moments—can see a possibility of hope.

Maya Angelou

Children—living and breathing. A gift. A piece of yourself. A piece of your mate. Hopefully, the best part of the both of you.

Then there are children who don't quite make it into your arms—without a name, a face, a bedroom with new curtains. They slip in and out of your life so quietly, without ever looking into your eyes and seeing the love there. The ache, the sorrow of losing them.

Nicole was yearning for another child, but by 1999 she had already endured three miscarriages, the last one induced by a ruptured cyst. Racing her to the emergency room, I was met at the doors by hospital staff, and she was quickly taken into surgery. While she was undergoing that procedure, the doctors discovered a second uterus that was the cause of the string of painful miscarriages. It was as if one healthy uterus had an evil twin.

But which one was which?

Within her, there was a healthy uterus able to carry to term and another unhealthy one that refused to keep the baby safe. They just couldn't identify the culprit. When they left both undisturbed for fear of making a horrible mistake, Nicole began to recover, at least physically.

It was a year and a half later when Nicole became pregnant again. And as the months went by, we both marveled and held our breath as her baby bump grew. She could feel it moving. The baby was alive and thriving! Its heart continued to beat as it carried our hopes and dreams with it—that second child on its way to us.

Nicole was five months pregnant when that precious heart stopped beating.

It's hard to put into words the despair and torment Nicole was experiencing. And it was difficult for me to be there emotionally for her because I had yet to be liberated from emotional incarceration. I was physically there, and my heart was broken, but I just did not know how to express my feelings. So, as most men would, I dismissed the pain and checked out.

Our child was too big for a D&C. Nicole would endure four days of injections in an attempt to dilate her cervix to induce labor. Nearly one hundred hours of grief, anguish, and unrelenting pain as they tried to separate mother from child—the child we so desperately wanted.

With the failure of the injections came a procedure to manually stretch her cervix. And whether it was improperly sterilized instruments or her body rebelling against a foreign object breaking in, an infection invaded her abdominal cavity. Strong antibiotics were pumped into Nicole's system, and the overload of medication nearly shut down her kidneys. With options running out, she was taken into surgery for a last-resort C-section.

It was during that surgery that they would finally know which uterus was unhealthy. The surgeon asked me for permission to remove it, and I gave it. The uterus and our beloved unborn child were taken together.

Our baby was gone.

The stress and sadness that came with each miscarriage stripped our hope little by little. With this last blow, I wasn't sure whether we would ever rebound. Nicole's doctors warned that she needed to wait, heal, and then see. But her mom and dad, myself, and even Alexis didn't want her to try again. To us, the danger outweighed the precarious reward.

As Nicole recovered at home for the next six weeks, I got a phone call from her as I was driving home after laying tile one day.

"Jason, I need to talk to you," she said, almost tearfully.

My nerves rattled. *Lord, don't let it be another complication …*

"What happened, Cole?" I could scarcely disguise my concern, nor did I feel the need to. She was my everything.

"Members from Rosedale brought us food tonight," she said, with her voice cracking slightly. "When I let them in and saw the food, I started crying. Then they prayed over me, hugged me, and left. Jason, the Holy Spirit told me that I should be at Rosedale."

Sometimes too many discouragements can become your normal. But just when you get used to the idea, something wonderful happens. A blessing occurs. It was another nod from Yah, speaking directly to my wife through His Spirit. And along with relief was a pride I felt in Nicole for receiving that message. It warmed me; it convinced me that patience is one of God's graces we should embrace with both arms. Nicole began attending Rosedale so consistently that I had to remind her to visit her parents at New Saint Mark from time to time.

Two working together to truly become one.

15

THE FORTITUDE TO FORGIVE

The weak can never forgive. Forgiveness is the attribute of the strong.

Mahatma Gandhi

In the midst of any storm, music remained my sanctuary. It was that love and passion that was best able to reach the lost, and it inspired me to launch a Christian hip-hop label called Yunion Records—the perfect counter to the multitude of negative influences of the secular hip-hop culture. But like any great love, it would take time to develop and establish itself. I stayed with my construction company to keep life afloat.

The same can be said for the patience needed in our human relationships as well. Those also need time to grow and mature.

Nicole and I were still struggling. Though we were now attending the same church, we viewed Scripture through different-colored lenses. At times, I felt disrespected by her denial to see things my way. She also refused to submit to my spiritual leadership. What I considered compromise, Nicole deemed common Christianity. It kept pushing us against each other, and no man likes to feel pushed. If I were ever feeling deflated at home, Powerhouse Gym pumped me back up.

This was the ultimate space where men went to blow off steam and decompress. We all bench-pressed weights to shrug off our mental burdens and to build back self-esteem. My workout crew consisted of about six other men, the main two being Darryl "Big D" Jackson and Edwin "Pig" Fowler. No other crew could have been tighter; we were medicine for one another, as close as comrades can be.

Darryl stood six feet, two inches tall and weighed in at an impressive 255 pounds of solid muscle. Big D was legendary for being one of the few men at Powerhouse who could pick up and press 200-pound dumbbells. He could also bench-press 315 pounds for twenty-rep sets. He was a machine; the perfect workout partner to inspire you to go the extra mile. He was easy to like as a friend and even easier to love as a brother.

On Sundays, we worked our legs. I was big on legs and endurance, so I would squat 315 pounds for five sets of fifteen reps. When someone would take too long on their set, he'd say, "Yo, there's a time limit!" which always pulled a smile out of me. He also referred to dumbbells under fifty pounds as "baby rattles." But that was Big D. He encouraged everyone but sadly couldn't express his own pain or struggles. He hid his stress behind that great big smile and physique.

After the 8:00 a.m. church service, I would meet D and Pig at the gym, and we'd hit it hard before going to get roasted chicken and watch the Detroit Lions. Thinking about that tasty ritual makes me long for those days—to go back in time and enjoy another Sunday with my boys. It was the start of a fifteen-year friendship with Big D. At the time, I didn't realize that those Sundays with me were actually "church" for D and Pig. You never know how you're affecting those around you. The things you say and do—they can and do reflect Christ without you knowing it. You may not notice, but *others* notice.

———— • ————

Then I met a woman. I did *not* have an affair.

Just someone to talk to about the Most High and the challenges that come with modeling a godly life. Strange to think I didn't see Satan's trap as it was unfolding. I wasn't even physically attracted to her; she was just a compassionate ear that listened, the way Delilah listened to Samson. A lot of men would consider it a nonissue, but I'm thankful that Yah would set me straight on that. I hadn't committed adultery, and I planned on keeping it that way until death or divorce.

As time went by, the woman hired me to tile her bathroom floor. One of my closest friends, Vic, went with me to help put together the estimate. After we finished with the estimate, we went our separate ways. A few minutes later, Vic left a joking comment about the woman on my voice mail.

"Hey, you gone holla at her?" he quipped.

That was so Vic, and I never deleted the message because it didn't mean anything to me.

When the job was completed, the woman and I still talked almost every day on the phone about the usual things—everyday life, church, Christianity. That was all. Completely innocent by most standards.

But not all.

When Nicole decided to check my voice mail—my wife and I (to this day) have an open-door policy regarding passwords—she heard Vic's message. Well, as you can imagine, all hell broke loose. And though I knew what I had and hadn't done, it was impossible for me to prove my innocence.

Nicole packed all my clothes and put them next to the door.

Why didn't I try harder?

Instead of fighting for my marriage, I allowed my emotions to take the fight out of me. I rented a U-Haul and moved back to my mother's house the same day. A very regretful Vic helped me move and even apologized to Nicole, explaining that it was all in jest. But the emotional damage had already been done. I didn't know how to cry or how to express my emotions to Nicole. That in itself did as much damage as the alleged offense.

Divorce seemed to be the next evolution, the easy way out.

The whole incident was more than I could take. There I was again, Mr. Ministry looking like a hypocrite. I still wanted my family, but I'd have to confront this head-on for any hope of beginning the healing of my wife's heart or restoring what I had lost so unexpectedly.

Stepping in to help with damage control, Pastor Dennis asked whether I would be willing to have a meeting with Nicole and the "other woman" to get it cleared up. It was the perfect remedy, so I was all for it.

After the woman told the truth about our friendship, I looked at Nicole and said, "I love you, and nothing happened between this woman and me." Right then, the tears began to flow. It was the first time I'd ever cried in front of Nicole.

It was a big deal.

It's probably the most vulnerable state for men and one that felt so unnatural yet unavoidable. It's called the process of healing. A transparency that reveals true intentions. A part of me was embarrassed. Growing up, I was taught to never be emotional in front of a woman. That they would inevitably use it against you. But let me tell you something: I'd also never felt release like that—grief, regret, love out in the open. All of it.

And when it was over, I felt *free*.

As I mentioned, many men, even some of my friends, don't consider a platonic relationship with a woman to be a problem. But I believe having a relationship with anyone of the opposite sex without your spouse's permission *is* wrong, and it can create an opportunity for the Devil to enter your marriage and cause all kinds of confusion and strife.

After Nicole and I made it through the worst of it, a sadness still remained. I knew Nicole and I still weren't at the place of reconciliation, but my soul was at peace. The tears I shed in front of my wife were just the start of a more open Jason. And in the coming years, Yah would teach me the blessing of being able to cry in front of and with my queen and would lead me to true liberation.

That first Christmas without my family was devastating. I remember the nights leading up to Christmas Eve when I would sit out in front of our home, crying as I looked through the window at the decorated Christmas tree. Sometimes I gathered the courage to walk up to get a closer view of Alexis playing in the living room. I'd stand there contemplating whether to ring the doorbell, but I never did. I simply got in the car and drove back to my mother's house, saddened and heartbroken.

Instead of enduring Christmas without my family, I chose to attend a Christian conference for young adults called IMPACT. That particular year, it was being held in Atlanta. I boarded the bus, praying that I would hear a word from Yah once I got there.

The conference was powerful, and my faith was renewed! But what happened next was completely unexpected. Nicole caught a flight to Atlanta to be with me. She arrived a few days after Christmas while Alexis spent time with my mother.

We talked all that night, and I apologized again, promising never to hurt her that way in the future.

Why couldn't we have left well enough alone?

But years of wounds can sometimes outmatch the best intentions. Then *bam*! Another argument. I know what you're thinking: *Been there, done that!* And no, it didn't fix a thing. At that point, we both said our marriage was over. We agreed that when we got back to Detroit, we would file for divorce.

What was it again about "what God has joined together, let no one separate" (Mark 10:9 NIV)? There had to be a way to mend our differences, but for the life of us—and our daughter—we couldn't find it.

Even though the IMPACT New Year's celebration was awesome, Nicole and I didn't talk to one another the remainder of our time in Atlanta. We boarded the group bus back to Detroit and still didn't speak. It was as if all the years of knowing her—since childhood, in some form or another—ended in a muted stalemate. Like strangers without a past. This was *not* what Yah had in mind for us. And as I sat in my seat, the Holy Spirit spoke to me.

"Jason, there will always be problems, but this is your wife. Reach over and take her hand."

Man, talk about a war within! The Spirit was like, "Do it!" But my flesh/soul was like, "No, she'll reject you. Don't do it!"

As I fought through my fear of rejection to obey the Spirit, I reached over for Nicole's hand … and she squeezed mine. And in that, a silent yet steadfast agreement to fight for our marriage was made.

Just because marriage is sometimes difficult doesn't mean we give up.

———— • ————

It was a Saturday morning in 2003 when I saw my dad's name on the caller ID. I gladly answered the phone, expecting a happy conversation that would get us caught up with each other and possibly get something scheduled on the calendar. Why else would he be calling?

A son can dream.

Launching into a tirade of questions, he accused me of stealing his credit card. At first, I thought he was kidding, but after a few seconds, I realized he was dead serious. I tried to stay cool.

"Why would you think I would steal from you?" I calmly asked him.

"Who in the [expletive] else could have done it?" he replied, cutting through all my defenses.

It was tough to keep my composure while listening to false allegations, but I managed it. Up until the point when he said he had his wife file a police report against me. Then I came unglued!

After all the years he tore me down, ignored me, or just wasn't there, he pulled this! Despite his attendance at my wedding and despite his struggle with Parkinson's, the idea that perhaps his conscience was finally giving him a new and grateful perspective was nothing more than a pipe dream. After everything we had been through together, he still hadn't changed.

But *I* had.

I wasn't about to let him get away with blaming me for something I didn't do, much less something that went against every conviction I had in Christ. It was an assault on my very character and faith.

Where I summoned the courage to curse out the man I feared more than God, I'll never know, but I did it! It was terrifying and liberating all at the same time. It's true he was never there for me, and the only difference now was that I said it out loud—to him. Without apology or regret, now he knew I was affected by it.

Afterward, I felt convicted that it was wrong to curse him, but I was finally free from decades of verbal oppression.

It wasn't until after I received an alarming call from my stepmother, Betty, years later that I would see my father again. And I would find that his Parkinson's had progressed to the point of leaving him bedridden and helpless.

"Honour thy father and thy mother" (Ex. 20:12 KJV) was the commandment Yah had been bringing to my mind for days prior to that call from her. It speaks to how much family means to Him. He was preparing me days in advance, making sure I would respond in a way that would bring glory to Himself. Love—sacrificial and persevering—through years of suffering and abuse. *His* love is able to do all things, if only we follow His example.

But how can you honor someone who has hurt you so much?

I would show him how.

After I rang the doorbell, I was greeted by Betty with a smile and a hug. She guided me to the room my father was resting in and said, "Oliver, guess who's here?"

No response.

My father was always a strong man, but as I sat down next to him, he looked so feeble and weak. It was enough to bring me to my knees in tears beside his bed. I wept as I rubbed his forehead, finally seeing what he truly was. What we all are. What Yah fashioned us from and what we will return to. Dust.

Then he opened his eyes and smiled. Smiled ... at me.

"Hey," he said with a glint in his eyes.

"Hey," I replied, soothing his anxious brow.

Tears, a cocktail of anger, bitterness, anguish, yearning, love, forgiveness, reconciliation. They can heal invisible wounds, water the driest soul, and wash away decades of pain. When shed from the purest place, they are the quickest way back to peace that I know of.

Love is the answer. It's always been the answer.

It was as if the combination of those unfettered tears and the revelation that my father had only a short time left to live started a chain reaction, purging our hearts and preparing the way ahead.

16

IT'S OKAY TO CRY

Never trust a warrior who cannot cry.

Irish proverb

Bottling emotions is a dangerous thing—when life shakes you and pops your top, you'll explode instead of pour.

In 2004 Yunion Records label got a national distribution deal with the first all-female compilation titled *The H.E.R. Project— Healing through Evangelism & Rhymes*. Things were slowly starting to move along with the help of Ronald Lee Jr., who not only was an executive producer but also recruited the female rappers. He would go on to be The Yunion's nonprofit program manager and remains a constant source of motivation and encouragement in my life.

While still operating my construction company, I produced music that made waves in the Christian hip-hop industry with songs like "My Story" on the Stellar Award winner Da'T.R.U.T.H's debut album *Moment of Truth*, which received the attention of platinum gospel artist

Kirk Franklin. The Yunion had the attention of everyone in Christian hip-hop, and our website was a popular destination for mature young Christians seeking culturally relevant articles, devotions, and forum discussions. We challenged them to "carry their cross" instead of just wearing one around their neck. We soon made our way into the public school system, shining the light but without proselytism.

All the while, martial arts was still in my veins. My journey through martial arts took me through boxing, judo, aikibujutsu, hapkido, iaido, and my current favorite, Brazilian Jujitsu. But it wasn't until I encountered the masterful teachings of Kajana Cetshwayo that I finally saw my greatest enemy—my inner me—my soul, the seat of my emotions, that which wars against Yah's Spirit within me. I was a subdued slave to my soul, double-minded and emotionally unstable.

But this was about to change.

In the winter of 2004 I attended a kenpo exhibition. I was leery at first because the kenpo I had seen was robotic and not practical for surviving in the streets of Detroit. But I quickly realized this was not the kenpo I had seen.

The chief instructor, Kajana Cetshwayo, was a legend with a plethora of stories that intrigued me, from his students raiding and shutting down crack houses, to purging drug dealers from the community, to being a buffer between the community and the police to reestablish peace in Detroit after the riots. Chief, as we called him, was a Vietnam veteran, and his heart was hardwired for survival.

To this day, I have never seen that kind of intensity practiced in the arts. He and his instructors presented attacks with real knives, choke defenses, gun takeaways—every scenario you would face in the street. As I watched the demonstration—the danger it involved—it brought a deluge of emotions to the surface. I was all in and signed up that day!

Within the first year of training, I saw lips busted, teeth loosened, bones broken, and hands cut from failed knife attack maneuvers. While sparring, I dislocated my index finger where it laid horizontally, crossing my middle finger. But instead of sitting me out, Chief popped the bone back into place and told me to continue fighting.

Chief was a warrior, and like most young men who desire a man to challenge them without condemnation, I eagerly continued.

For me, training under Chief was as much a psychological education as it was a training in the arts. Wading through past anxiety and anger (though my dad and I were on speaking terms) was like drilling for oil. And once that underground reservoir was tapped, I needed a safe space to be transparent and vulnerable.

My biblical counselors and my pastors were always available to hash over the disappointments and long-standing aggravation that was creeping to the surface, but nothing really worked. It wasn't until I met Chief that I first heard the term *passive aggressive* and how it can affect a man. The Passive Aggressive Conflict Cycle (PACC) was the perfect description for what I was experiencing—the symptoms of buried rage.

It was also going to take time to work through a bitter past. And it would take place not in the shelter of a pastor's office or a one-on-one lunch meeting but on the dojo floor, fighting.

Punching, piercing, kicking ... with a flurry of blows, Chief kept striking. It felt as if I couldn't get one decent strike in. With frustration mounting, something suddenly clicked. I ignored the flurry of blows, zoned in, and struck him in his jaw.

Laughing, he said, "You come off all gentle, but when something makes you angry—watch out—you do whatever it takes to destroy the threat, regardless of whether your actions are detrimental to you or others."

It was the "sledgehammer and mosquito" mentality I'd adopted after losing a fight. He had put his finger right on it.

He continued, "It's like a shark who tastes blood in the water. He loses sight of all that's around him to focus in on killing his prey. But his tunnel vision makes him vulnerable to the hunter with a speargun, aiming at him."

Needless to say, the illustration proved his point. We bowed and resumed sparring.

Striking, striking, striking … another barrage of blows came at me, and again, I got mad and targeted his jaw. But in the process of trying to hit him, I lost sight of one of his blows, and before I knew it, he struck me in my solar plexus and I folded. It was a lesson on so many levels. I was reacting with the same aggression that spurred me to hold back with those in the world who upset me, then turn around and unleash on Nicole or Alexis at the slightest offense. The epiphany was the first of many before my training under Chief was over.

"You're not trying to hit me!" Chief said one day as we were sparring. Of course, I thought he was tripping. Then before we could get a good flow sparring again, he put his face directly in front of my thrusting fist, and I subconsciously veered it away from his head. I was speechless! *Why did I do that?*

What was that? I wondered, stunned that my motor skills had that kind of reflex. But it was not my body but my mind that wasn't allowing me to hurt him.

"Jason, you're three times my size, but you're not imposing your will on me. You think your size is your problem, but in this situation, it should be my problem. If the Creator made you dominant, then you should dominate for Him. Anything less is disobedience. You don't have to try to be humble. You either are or you're not."

For some reason, my life had seen more than its share of loss and heartache. Over and over, again and again, a type of posttraumatic stress disorder had settled into my bones, and to this day, at times I still expect things to go wrong before they can go right. That's what happens when you get shaken too many times. Up to bat with a fear of hitting the fence. Too many strikeouts will keep the best slugger from swinging.

———— • ————

That same year, Big D was in need of some extra income. Vic and I hired him as a laborer for construction jobs, and it was great having two of my favorite men working with me. I trusted them. They were family.

I was in the studio recording the afternoon Vic and D were working a demolition project. The phone rang, and seeing the call was from Vic, I didn't think it was urgent so I let it go to voice mail.

Then, it rang again.

Like before, it was Vic. I stopped the session, feeling uneasy. When I answered, Vic's voice was far from his usual funny, light-hearted tone.

"Jay, Big D passed out," Vic said in a panic.

"Okay, how's he doing now?" I asked, thinking it was probably a simple case of dehydration.

"He's not breathing. I tried CPR, but he's not breathing!"

Big D was a gentle giant. With so much time spent together—working out at the gym, doing construction jobs, and enjoying those precious Sundays—my mind couldn't wrap itself around the thought of anything happening to him. Another tragedy within my family was not a possibility. There was no way this could end badly, and I refused to believe the worst.

I rushed to the job site, but Nicole called while I was en route. She said the ambulance had already taken Big D to the emergency room and to meet him there. As a registered nurse, Nicole knew more about physical distress than most, and I didn't like the hesitation in her voice.

The ambulance was pulling into the ER when I arrived, and I ran to D's side. His arms dangled over the stretcher as it was lowered out. He wasn't moving. The man that could press 300-plus pounds over his head didn't move a muscle. Unconscious, unresponsive, *helpless*. It puts the fear in you seeing someone that size on his back. He set the bar physically, encouraged me emotionally, and stood next to me at my wedding. He was as sturdy as they came.

In a matter of minutes, the waiting room was packed with D's friends and family anxiously awaiting news of his condition. It says a lot about a man who can fall down and have so many people suddenly there to help pick him up. It speaks to his character and compassion for others.

That was Big D.

We waited for word, and still nothing. Stepping outside for some fresh air, I needed to inhale—deeply. To feel oxygen in my lungs, to remind myself that life was all around me, spontaneous but steady, fragile yet still formidable. Flesh and blood, famous for its resilience. I didn't want to consider that life could go from being unquestionably here and now to inconceivably there and gone.

My friend was enormous, strong, and so able to weather the afflictions of life. Nothing could bring down Big D. Nothing!

As I walked around outside the hospital entrance for a couple of minutes, I tried to gather my thoughts and the strength to walk back inside. A deep breath, an exhale, and a silent prayer for D's recovery.

When I returned to the waiting room, I saw Vic on his hands and knees. Darryl's mother, girlfriend, ex-wife, and two daughters were crying. Big D had died of a massive heart attack. The man with so much love in him was taken down by his own heart. He was forty-one years old.

The tears crept closer and closer to the surface, leaving me stripped and vulnerable. Another funeral to attend. Another friend to bury. Another wound to heal. Another hole in me to fill.

Before Darryl's memorial service, I felt like crying. I even told Pastor Haman Cross Jr., who was doing the eulogy. I'm so glad I did. He replied as if Yah whispered directly to him.

"Jason, *cry.*"

And I did. I allowed my soul to grieve, and that simple act of showing emotion gave me the power to speak at the funeral so boldly it gave many of our gym friends closure to D's death. And as I stood in the mausoleum, weeping over Darryl's coffin, Pastor Dennis reached down and wiped the tears from the casket with a rose, then laid it on top.

"Jason, it's time to go."

The Bible says when Lazarus died, "Jesus *wept*" (John 11:35). It is the shortest yet arguably the most powerful Scripture when it comes to Yahushua modeling the vulnerability of tears and strength in a natural response to great heartache. Yet Christ did it knowing He would soon raise His friend from the grave. Still, His gut reaction was necessary to heal—to feel hurt and cry is an important part of that process.

Ungrieved losses are unhealed wounds that eventually get infected with depression, anxiety, and fear, just to name a few harmful side effects. Christ let Himself, as well as those around Him, mourn as a soul should. Yah knows that in order for our souls to recover from earthly pain, we have to express it. It's the human thing to do.

After Big D's death, a single glance at a lightweight dumbbell brought a sentimental chuckle and lump to my throat. "Baby rattles" do that to me.

Baby rattles ...

With another life passing out of this world, another one steps in to fill it. An infant happily playing, a toddler taking his or her first step, a little child within a loving home.

Would I ever know that feeling again?

17

FREEING MY FATHER

Every saint has a past, and every sinner has a future.
Oscar Wilde, *A Woman of No Importance*

My heart wanted a son.

Doesn't every man? Is it lost identity, a chance to make things right, or just plain ego? Maybe it's all three, but what really mattered now was that my wife had been through enough.

Nicole's pregnancy in 1995 with our daughter, Alexis, wasn't without its share of close calls. And after so many miscarriages, the doctors told us it would be too dangerous for us to have any more children. In 2002, during her fifth pregnancy and miscarriage, the doctors gave her medication that ultimately caused her uterus to rupture. Within twenty-four hours, she was back in the hospital for emergency surgery with another long recovery ahead.

Her petite little body had been through so much. Did we have the right to believe our dream of having a son would ever come true?

After the last miscarriage and hysterectomy of the dual (unhealthy) uterus, Nicole returned to school and got her MBA in health care management with plans to start her own health center. She graduated in 2004. What can I say ... *I married a winner!*

By 2005 the construction industry had taken a major hit, and the housing market was collapsing. Many of my friends in the field had to shut down their businesses to find different work. And it appeared that Yah was moving me into a new season as well.

With my main laborer, Kyle, taken out of commission because of a car accident, I was faced with a dilemma. In my discouragement, I prayed for guidance, and the very next day I got a call from my dear friend, Mike Tenbusch, the COO of the new but highly acclaimed charter school, University Preparatory Academy (UPA).

He needed two things: security to address the rise in gang activity and a mentor to help students combat its influences and stress. When Mike had me come in and speak to two rival gangs in hope of defusing an escalating conflict, my first question to the group was one that I could have answered myself, but I wanted to hear from them.

"How many of y'all have your fathers in your house?"

I knew the question would organically bring up all kinds of emotions and hopefully shine a light on why they joined a gang in the first place. Within minutes of sharing my own emotional pain of an absentee father, eyes began to swell with tears. By the end of the session, hardened juveniles were apologizing to one another, giving one another dap, and hugging it out.

It was such a powerful moment when I saw myself in those boys. They banded together in gangs to feel loved, admired, and affirmed. I could see how, like me, they fought their isolation and loneliness in numbers. They knew what it was like to intentionally fail a test just to get attention. To react in ways that opposed their moral code of conduct just to appease their peers. The mental issues that ran rampant as a direct result of unaddressed anger and emotions. It was all there.

Yah was doing a work—in them *and* in me.

By my second visit to the school, I had fallen in love with UPA. Along with mentoring and security, I also maintained the school facility with the skills that came so naturally to me in construction. The institute's philosophy was to create a campus as aesthetically pleasing as Disney World, giving the students a sense of value, of feeling special. And it worked!

It wasn't an easy decision to leave LME—the successful business I had started out of my garage—but I reminded myself why I was called to UPA and whom I was representing. I was Yah's hands, feet, mouth, arms, and legs. His love.

Looking back, I can see plainly that my knowledge in building was needed far more in the construction of young men of valor than of houses made of wood. Any one of those boys could be His future temple, His fortress, His home to inhabit. And I was assisting the Chief Carpenter.

The thought of providing security for more than three hundred students after school each day was overwhelming. There were so many kids and only me to provide a safe place as the campus grounds cleared. How would I ever get the job done?

I prayed, "How on earth can I do this, Yah? I'm only one man, and there are so many holes for outside gangs or troublemakers to enter. Please, help me."

As if standing next to me, His Holy Spirit whispered, "You are my David and they are my sheep. Watch them with all diligence, and the wolves will stay at bay."

I started to patrol the area in an X pattern through the crowd of kids, not only to appear vigilant but also to keep an eye on the students most likely to start a fight. Conquering the human psyche has more power than sparring with the body, and I purposefully intruded into the lives and minds of the negative influencers.

Not your typical "rent-a-cop" with a wrinkled uniform and protruding belly, but six feet, one inch of ripped muscle weighing in at 230 pounds. My gear was head-to-toe black army fatigues with black lace-up boots. Before my arrival, UPA had experienced plenty of fights. During my two years at UPA, there were none.

My "relational security" approach was a success, to the point where students would alert me prior to a conflict in order for it to quickly be resolved. Because of my ability to calm down boys, even those from outside the school who made a special trip to attack a student would often return just to talk to me about life.

When you're confronted with Christlike compassion, it's very hard to resist. And the Christian hip-hop music I played in the gym while spotting football players lifting weights didn't hurt either. I'd hear, "What's that song, Mr. Wilson?" and I'd hand them a CD.

But at the end of the day when the music fell silent and the students went home, the pressures in their personal lives continued. There had to be an answer to the growing hopelessness and arrested emotional development in these kids.

Beyond music production and recording, The Yunion needed to expand into mentoring services. But that would cost money. It was then that I decided to establish the label as a nonprofit to gain funding. It would take an additional two years to acquire the grant, but we got it.

The Yunion would eventually reach over ten thousand Metro Detroit youth with innovative prevention programming, engaging workshops, assemblies, and conferences. Not a bad legacy to leave behind.

But who thinks about leaving—until your ticket has been punched?

———— • ————

His sheets were as worn and creased as the lines in his eighty-year-old face.

My father was now bedridden from the devastating effects of Parkinson's. With my twice-weekly visits, I was spending more time with my dad now than at any other stage of my life. And though I relished those frequent visits, I detested the punishing circumstances that were responsible. The tremors that were his constant unwelcome companion. The loss of his independence. The stench of the nursing home—a bizarre mix of antiseptic, urine, and death—was the odor of an uneasy context.

Like a big plate of soul food, your favorite cologne, or even sweaty sneakers, smells store passion, emotions, and memories. My dad's smell was ironic. A combination of disinfectant and decay. His hourglass was running out but still with plenty in it to afford him time to think.

Without a body to enable him to enjoy an afternoon of bowling or to stand for hours at his barber's chair visiting with patrons and friends; without the stamina of a young man's sex drive to seduce women, stroking his all-important male ego; without a place left to hide, my dad lay confined to a bed of regret, replaying his life one victory and one defeat at a time.

"Dad, is there anything you want me to do, any promise I can make?"

The question came after hearing a sermon about fulfilling a promise to your parent before he or she dies. Whether your parents did you right or did you wrong, you're still in control of how you respond.

"I want you to preach the gospel, and I want to hear your first message."

For a minute, I thought I was hearing things. What did he know about the gospel? Then he told me about the Most High's calling on his life to preach the good news to the lost. But he emphatically told Yah that He had the wrong man for the job. I couldn't believe it. This was my father we're talking about. The same man who verbally abused me, emotionally scarred me, and abandoned me to my own devices.

I learned later that it was the affair of his own father, an ordained minister, that caused my dad's anger toward and intolerance of the hypocritical church. And because of it, he would never answer the call. But "never" is debatable, until your last breath is on its way out.

It was an unbelievable request but one I intended to fulfill. That year, I spoke at church for the very first time. It was taped, and with the recording in hand, I raced back to my dad for him to hear it. I placed headphones over his ears, and he smiled as he listened to his son living out the Most High's calling.

He heard the nerves in my voice but chuckled and said, "Boy, you sound nervous, but you did good. I'm so proud."

Proud ... of me. How can five little letters mean so much?

He bragged to the nurses, "My son is preaching at church!"

It was almost too wonderful to accept. My father was actually boasting about me—about preaching, no less. Unbelievable!

Later in the week, it got even weirder when my dad asked me whether he could pray before I left. I didn't think he knew *how* to pray, but he did. And when he was finished and we said amen, I went to release his hand, but he wouldn't let go.

"Your turn," he said.

So I prayed, and we went back and forth for about five minutes. I was blown away. When we were through, I just looked at him—right into him—and spoke the thing that truly needed to be said.

"Dad, thank you for being a great father." Then I kissed him on the forehead.

As I was turning to walk away, I noticed a tear rolling down his cheek, then another one, then streams. No way could I walk out on him. No way could I deny myself this kind of memory.

I sat back down and wiped his tears ... and stayed.

What a strange reversal of fortune. What an incredible gift of unexpected tenderness. He may have felt he was undeserving, and that could be true, but it didn't matter to me. He struck out at the plate of my life seemingly every time he went to bat, but he hit a home run when it counted the most. He swung for the fences and hit it out of the park.

I realized that affirmation was something he needed as well. Every man needs it.

He then looked at me so genuinely, his expression so unfamiliar to me, he looked like a different person. Then came the olive branch I had been waiting for all my life.

"I love you, son."

I rested my head on his chest, and we cried until our souls were empty. He finally said the words. He was finally free, and I had been given the key.

Strongholds were being taken out and spiritual highways that would bring in huge blessings were being laid down. And I would experience more miracles in his last days, answers to prayer, and extra time to share.

I visited Dad more frequently after that, always with a pen, pad, and my BlackBerry in hand, taking notes and allowing Yah to heal us both.

On January 15, 2007, Yah said it was time for my father to go home, and he answered the call. I rushed to the hospital and kissed him one last time before they took away his body.

"Dad, I won't let you down. I will preach the gospel, and the bowling pins you left standing in life, I'll knock 'em all down."

Suffering—it chips away at, massages, and softens the hardest of hearts. It opens our eyes to the paper-thin barrier between us and the world to come. It clears out pettiness and prioritizes those things that matter most. It brings us down from our haughty heights.

Before Dad took his last breath, he said, "If I could do it all over, I would."

May we all learn from the mistakes we make in life, while we still have a life to live.

18

PREPARATION
FOR THE PURGE

*Sometimes God calms the storm, but sometimes God
lets the storm rage and calms His child.*

Author Unknown

And the rain fell.

It fell like tears flowing from heaven's gate in my father's wake as his body laid still in his grave. So much rain, so many tears. The funeral took place in Chipley, Florida, where my father was born and would finally rest. I trusted that Yah would bless him with peace, without guilt or condemnation. He had found his way home— physically and spiritually—as the downpour continued without the faintest sign of relief.

I was spellbound by the casket, my feet hugged by the damp grass. I could have cried there all day, but the rain ... the rain. At the end, I think we're given the opportunity to release our grief and all the tears that we didn't find the time or strength to shed in life. But there does come a time when the water dripping down our faces is replaced by the sun of what's to come. And we should let it.

As we all left the cemetery, neither my tears nor the drizzle let up. But at least my feet were moving. I longed to stay behind, to have just a few more private minutes with my dad. We had finally found resolution and an appreciation for our own breakability. We were at last human together and so broken. I wished we had the chance to go back—to break free—and believe in each other from the start. What an amazing relationship that would have been.

What *could* have been.

Now there was only soggy ground and the dismal faces of those who loved him and whom he loved in his own flawed way. Sinking feet and spirits left him behind in closing commemoration of his eighty years on earth.

Sleep well, Dad, and I'll see you on the other side.

And as the hearts of two brothers were connected in life, so too were they connected in death. As the family gathered at the church for the repast, my cousin began to wail and scream. He had just received a call informing him of his own father's death. My uncle's body was still at the house when we arrived, and we prayed together before the undertaker took him away. The timing was shocking. As the entire family from other states had converged for my father's funeral, we were all present to pray for his brother now on his way to be with my father.

It was then that I caught the magnitude of my own spiritual lineage. My dad's entire family minus only a few were ministers and pastors. Even my grandmother had become a minister in the days when women were expected to stay quiet in church. My father's funeral was held at Uncle Price's parish, and it was astonishing to find such a gold mine of spiritual heavyweights in my own bloodline.

———— • ————

Standing in a hot shower after we got back to Detroit, I heard the Holy Spirit say, "You do understand that after you, there are no more."

Would the father-son lineage be broken with me?

After I dried off, I walked into our family room where Nicole was sitting and asked, "Do you pray for us to have another baby, specifically a boy?"

She replied, "Yes, I always wanted to give you a son."

I told Nicole I didn't want to lose her but Yah had prompted me to pray for a son. Asking for such a gift wasn't something I took lightly. There was nothing I wanted more at that point than a baby boy. But having watched Nicole experience such agony to produce one child, I had resigned myself to buying a bullmastiff and naming him Son just to give me an excuse to use the word.

Even so, Nicole and I prayed together in faith that the Most High would allow her to conceive and bear a son. It was risky after the multiple miscarriages and emergency surgeries, but we continued to lift up our request, and two weeks later, Nicole was pregnant with our son.

I was terrified and thrilled at the same time!

But we had traveled this road before and through much—both emotional and physical—and always seemed to wind up at a dead end. We took things slow, ever mindful that the Lord giveth and the Lord taketh away (see Job 1:21). But in all things, He is the boss.

I wish I could say that the rose He handed us was thorn free, but I've learned that the most precious gifts come with a hefty price tag. The pregnancy was not uneventful, and at the five-month mark, Nicole's appendix burst, which resulted in an emergency appendectomy. Our doctor had to remove the uterus—with its precious cargo—in order to operate. It was then placed back inside Nicole. They warned us that it was possible our boy would have Down syndrome and to prepare for it.

On September 24, 2007, our son was born prematurely but healthy. There he was in the flesh, four pounds, eleven ounces of little man looking at me with those familiar Wilson eyes and holding my finger with a superman grip. He made it to us, by the grace of Yah. He was with us!

Another downpour, another shower from heaven, this time watering a garden of joy. From my eyes that I never thought would see this miracle to be so blessed and to find such unspeakable happiness in this life. From a child who buried his emotions to a man crying at the sight of his newborn son's face, I was getting pretty good at letting it all hang out. Even the anesthesiologist started tearing up.

Yah had kept His promise. The father-son circle was safe. Suddenly those words He spoke to me on the heels of my father's funeral filled me with a sense of awe. It didn't have to end with me. I just needed to ask Him to remember His servant. As I prayed together with my prayer-warrior wife, He heard and answered us.

Incredibly, I was a father for the second time! And despite my own damaged upbringing, I was determined to be the best dad I could be. Was I perfect? No … what human is? But I knew what I *didn't* want to be, and that was a start. By example, my father had drawn the blueprint of what not to do, what not to say, and what not to place on a child.

Encouragement, guidance, and love would be the cornerstones that would enable my son to grow and thrive. Alexis may have had the better father physically, but my son would have the better father emotionally.

We named him Jason Jr.

———— • ————

It was now 2009, and still my emotions hindered the Most High's transformational power from moving through me. I felt it was obvious that I should pray for Him to break me. Think about it. Only when the wheat is cut down, *broken*, ground up, and baked in the fire is it ready to feed one or many.

So it was with me. So it is with you.

That summer, I was scheduled to have my shoulder repaired from a common gym injury. It was supposed to be a simple outpatient procedure, but the Holy Spirit forewarned me that my *breaking* was about to begin.

When the surgery was over, the doctors rolled me into recovery. All had gone well. The breaking of me didn't seem so bad after all.

Then the spinal block wore off.

Suddenly I became distressed and began thrashing like a drowning man. I couldn't breathe! I learned later that I had what's termed "flash pulmonary edema"—my lungs were filling with fluid.

The doctors rushed me back into surgery to intubate me. After two days in the ICU with a breathing tube down my throat, I was cleared to leave.

But as quickly as those storm clouds cleared, more dark skies appeared. The breaking process had just begun.

The mind is a complicated invention. At times, it's a blanket of warmth filled with memories you wrap around yourself to recall how you once were: how you swam the currents of commerce, went the extra mile for a friend, sang alone, danced in a crowd, played, laughed, loved. How you kept on task or lost track of time. How you did things right or how you could have *made* them right if only you had the time.

Time.

But then a fog rolls in and suddenly the mind loses its tracking device. Its bedrock of the past and all its colorful history begins to fade until all that's left is gray. Names, faces, places, years, months, days fall victim to the thickening mental mist of nothingness.

My great-aunt Carrie (sister of my grandmother and sister-in-law to my grandfather Estes Wright) was now living with my mother. She was elderly and needed a caretaker, and they passed the hours talking about old times until it became evident that it was too physically demanding on my mom. My mother was left with no choice but to put my great-aunt in a nursing home where she would be more comfortable.

Aunt Carrie was a beautiful soul. She was there with my grandfather Estes just before he took his last breath in that jail in Fort Pierce, Florida—his face bloodied, his body broken, his neck stretched and swollen. But Aunt Carrie went on to live a good long life. She was a jewel through her final days and, taking a turn for the worse, was not expected to live much longer. We called her son, who was living in Texas. He quickly boarded a flight to Detroit.

While he was still in the air above the clouds, Aunt Carrie left this world. Perhaps she passed him on the way up, but he never got to see his mother alive again.

Hours later, my cousin cried at her bedside on his knees. "I tried to make it, Mama! I tried to make it!"

It was an unbearable scene—a son tearful with remorse—as I watched and heard the Holy Spirit say to me, "Do you want this to be you?"

We have one birth mother. That's all we get. And once she's gone, there's no bringing her back. Yah willing, I would have all the time I needed to enjoy my mother's company, to say and do everything a son should, which included taking care of her in her old age. That was my wish and plan all along.

It's a plan so easily thought of yet difficult to accomplish as life takes over and pushes out our best intentions. Like most sons with families and responsibilities, I probably saw my mother once a week. It was Nicole who organized her medications, helped her pay her bills, and made a conscious effort to go by her house to check up on her.

My cousin stayed with my mom for two more days after Aunt Carrie passed. He cut the grass, washed her clothes, massaged her feet, and lavished attention on her. I don't know whether it was guilt from missing Aunt Carrie's passing, but anything my mother needed, he did.

In his faithful service to Mama, I was being shown how a son should treat his mother—gentle, thoughtful, present.

It was still dark outside when I picked up my cousin to catch his flight back to the Lone Star State. As we pulled away from the house, he hung his head out of the window, yelling, "I love you, Auntie!" The tears in his eyes were his sincerest testimony. "I love you, Auntie!" he shouted down the block. Then he turned and looked at me, saying, "Jason, never put anything over your mother. Love her with everything you got."

I knew he was right.

On the way back from the airport, I called my mother, crying. "Mom, I'm sorry! I haven't been a good son, but that's going to change today!" With a clear picture of commitment in my head, I would pick up where my cousin had left off.

Visiting three and four times a week, I mowed her lawn, cleaned the house, and spent quality time with Mama. I was the child who came into her life, giving her a renewed sense of purpose. Now she was the one giving me a new purpose. It was my privilege and her due reward.

However, aging is a challenge for the weak and for a warhorse like Etta Marie. She was getting up there, and I started to notice the telltale signs that the years were catching up with her. Dings and dents in her car began to appear as well as uncharacteristic forgetfulness about her meds and random responsibilities. I assumed it was all just part of the inevitable slowing of mind and body that none of us can escape.

But when Nicole noticed that Mama was getting lost while driving, I cringed at what had to happen next.

It was a tough day when I took my mother's car keys away—to the car I helped her purchase. She was peeved! It was the only new car she had ever owned, and for her own child to confiscate her keys was humiliating. Still, her rationality was intact, and she couldn't deny that it was probably for the best.

In that one decision came an altered state of affairs. Her compromised travel suddenly made me her taxi service. To the bank, to the post office, to JCPenney for a cotton summer dress. It was a classroom for compromise and a testing of the wills.

By far the most educational place in elder care was found on Wyoming Street, where I took my mother to grocery shop—better known as Kroger. With no more than a dozen items on her list, you would think thirty minutes would be plenty of time for that seemingly simple errand. Try an hour and a half.

Bless her, she would insist on inspecting every section of the store, every aisle—meat, dairy, produce, canned, boxed, bottled, endless options—but no additions were ever made to her fixed list of staples. Just the original ten to twelve mainstays that she had been buying since the dawn of time.

It would have been easy to get irritated and maybe even wait in the car, but the old impatient Jason was dying, and I mean that in the best sense. I started to actually enjoy our ninety-minute strolls through Kroger, and I could tell she enjoyed them too.

Mama also loved her garden; working in it was her respite after a cluttered day with too much stress. It was a place to relax, to create something beautiful, green, and serene. Then I started noticing her beloved yard growing a few extra weeds with parched areas and forgotten leaves. The immaculate grounds had fallen into disarray, which was not at all like my mother.

It was time—time to move Mama in with us. But we would need a bigger house.

Nicole and I closed the deal on the home that we had always dreamed about—a 3,600 square foot ranch-style house that included an in-law suite, where my mom would be comfortable without feeling too intrusive. It had a huge backyard for her to putter in, to landscape and grow her vegetables. Everyone has a passion, and I wanted to encourage hers.

Though the house needed a lot of work, my construction experience made it perfectly doable. Slowly the house was brought up to code, and we looked forward to the day we could all move in together. But with the complex renovations and our toddler, Jason, needing our attention, Nicole and I thought it would be best if Mama traveled to Atlanta to spend time with her best friend, Byrda, while I finished up the house.

Atlanta—ground zero for what would redefine the future of all of us for years to come.

19

THE CRUCIBLE

God raises the warrior through hardship.
John Eldredge, *Fathered by God Participant's Guide*

It was April 2010 at 10:00 a.m. when worlds collided.

Byrda was a longtime friend and ally of my mother throughout her life. For years, they had trusted each other with their struggles, war wounds, and countless secrets I will never fully know. And even when Byrda moved to Atlanta, the two stayed in touch, safe within the other's confidence.

I had sent my mom to Atlanta while I finished renovations on our new house. Because I had injured my knee, the work was moving a little slower than anticipated. But Mama had her best friend to spend time with while I completed the updates. With so much going on, it seemed like the perfect solution—until my mother screamed for the police as she ran out of the house and into the quiet neighborhood street.

On the day she was due to board her flight home to Detroit, I was eating breakfast with a pastor friend when I got a phone call. The second I said hello, I heard a woman screaming in the background. I had no idea it was Mama.

"Jason, I don't know what happened ... Marie just lost it!" The panic in Byrda's voice was palpable.

I could hear my mother shrieking, cursing out Byrda, and pleading for the neighbors to call the police.

"It came outta nowhere ... just flew into a rage, throwing and breaking things. Tell me what to do!"

This did *not* sound like my mom—damaging property and threatening her best friend. I immediately called my brother Sinclair, who was still living in Texas, and within minutes phoned Byrda back on a three-way line.

"Let me talk to my mom, Byrda!" I figured if she could just hear our voices, we could calm her down. As Byrda held out the phone, I heard her pleading with my mother.

"Marie, your sons are on the phone. Talk to Jason, Marie. Talk to Jason!"

When Mama finally took the phone from her, it frightened me. This wasn't the woman I had known for the last forty years. She was hysterical, paranoid, terrified. She was convinced Byrda was going to kill her.

Her history—decades of trauma she had kept locked away—had finally surfaced with a vengeance. Her mind could no longer filter her emotions or find solace in her selective memory. The fear and trepidation of untold suffering was now on full display.

By the grace of Yah, we were able to quell the hysteria, and she got on the plane back to Detroit. When she arrived, Nicole and I took her straight to the doctor, where we were told she would need twenty-four-hour supervised professional care. And as quickly as I digested the unsettling news, my dream of Mama living with us slipped away.

Now, instead of making my mother comfortable and well cared for in her old age as planned, we were suddenly scrambling to find a suitable assisted-living facility for her, and quickly. Not just any one, but one that felt like home with caring individuals and around-the-clock nursing staff.

With so many things on my plate—finishing house renovations, working The Yunion nonprofit, and being a present husband and father—I now had the daunting task of an elusive treasure hunt. It seemed that with every assisted-living home we looked at came dismal provision in an unsanitary environment. The conditions were appalling, and I was shocked that many of them were allowed to keep their licenses.

As Mama and I drove home one afternoon following an inspection of a potential future provider, she stared at me with steely eyes. "I wouldn't do *you* like this." I knew what she meant, and the thought had already crossed my mind.

She rocked back and forth in her seat and continued, "But it's okay, Jason. It's okay. But no one should abandon their mother."

Ouch! That hurt—to the core.

Deep inside, I believed she understood that I was doing the best I could, but the words still shot holes in me with the guilt that comes with being the primary decision maker. Every time I entertained the notion of having Mama stay with us—against the doctor's advice—I remembered the words she often said to me after I married Nicole.

"Jason, never put anyone over your family"—referring to Nicole, Alexis, and Jason—"not even me!"

"Mom, you *are* my family!" I would counter.

But her response never wavered. "No, I'm your mother; *they* are your family."

Mothers are a melting pot of the past, present, and future—an archive of copious recollections, celebrations, and longings neatly tucked away behind soft eyes. It was as if she could see what was coming way back then, giving me permission to do what was necessary now. Advice that she'd learned the hard way. And it was this wisdom that helped me carry on.

Life is filled with ironies. Some make you laugh, while others badger you till you cry. But they always teach something worth knowing.

———— • ————

We decided on an assisted-living home in a beautiful community just two minutes from our house. Huntington Woods was rated number nine on the *Forbes* friendliest towns list, and it was clean, picturesque, and full of life.[1] Unlike other places we had seen, it was soaked with the sounds of lively conversation and smelled of home cooking. Barbecued ribs, baked beans, mac and cheese, and collard greens were on the menu the day we took our tour—all Mom's favorites.

It did feel like home, and Mama seemed to love it as we did the walk-through. We checked her in despite my concerns about the price. With her fixed income, things were tight. But the owner, Kathy, crunched the numbers and made it work. She was a godsend, becoming a sister to me and a daughter to my mother. The perfect scenario.

The next day Mama woke up in her new room. The fairy dust had vanished, and all that was left was the stark reality that she wasn't with her family. By the time I got there, she was curled up on her bed like a little girl, weeping.

"What's wrong, Ma?" I asked.

"Jason, I just didn't think it would end like this."

My heart split wide open. "Mom, I'm trying to do the best I can."

"I know you are, Jason," she said and kept crying.

I stayed for a while, reassuring her that everything was going to be okay. She would make new friends, she would enjoy a lovely community of people her own age, and we would visit often and pick her up to spend time at our home. The words were true enough, but when spoken to a heartbroken woman who just wants to go home, they end up floating away on a cold, thin breeze.

I left beneath a cloud of melancholy that followed me to the car. I got in and shut the door, drenched in misery. But there was nothing I could do. As I looked out over my dashboard, willing myself to turn the key, my throat tightened as hot tears streamed down my cheeks. As a music producer, I was used to being the Mystro in charge, orchestrating the perfect song, beats, and sound that was under my direction. In the driver's seat! Well, I was still in the driver's seat, literally, but without a map, more lost than ever. My course uncertain.

I felt so alone. I could only imagine how lonely my mother felt, hugging her pillow and whispering to herself, "I want to go home."

What did the future look like? I have no shame in admitting to you that I was scared—of what my mother was facing and also for what lay ahead for me. Would I be able to hold up under the pressure, or would I cave? All I knew was that I didn't want to lose my mom's love and respect.

Kathy assured me that it would get easier for Mama with time. And it did … it just took a few years.

Beyond the daily visits to see her—once or twice a day—I found myself making additional trips just to put her at ease. It seemed that I was the only one she would listen to. As Mom's dementia progressed, so did her paranoia, depression, and anger. My personal life was in pieces: no hobbies, no hanging out. I had surrendered them to my first love—my mother. And since I was her only child living in Detroit, the brunt of the responsibility fell on me.

Sadly, my presence wasn't enough to stop her decline or even slow it down. Her disease was known not for its gentle progression but for its ruthless extremes.

Soon she was scuffling with her roommates, attempting to break the window to escape her "kidnappers," and insisting that someone call the police to save her. Mama finally even threatened to hurt herself and others. It seemed that it was always my mom creating the drama, which gave her the nickname "The Godmother," a sad spin on the brazen Marlon Brando classic.

As I began to study the despicable disease that was stealing my mother, I realized that the meds of a dementia patient should be reevaluated on a consistent basis—every six months. Kathy suggested that I send Mama to a geropsychiatric doctor, but I hesitated. This meant she would have to spend a week in the hospital psych unit— the same type of place I imagined Hannibal Lecter called home.

But after Mama threatened to kill her roommate, I had no choice but to take her for reevaluation.

The psychiatric ward was not at all what I had envisioned. It was a secure, clean area of the hospital with an exceptional staff. The doctors were kind and assured me that they would craft the best combination of medication for Mom's treatment. As I walked out, leaving my mother there, one of the nurses smiled and said, "Your mother is in a very safe place. She'll be fine."

I jokingly thought to myself, *Yeah, right. You don't know my mama!*

On the second day, a 2:00 a.m. call from the psych unit informed me that my mother had fallen trying to run away from a nurse, convinced he was trying to kill her. After stitching up Mama's eye, they would continue to sedate her and fine-tune an effective drug therapy.

It's true I had asked Yah to break my "old mold," but this was too much! Ideally, I'd have preferred to keep the wineskin intact. New wine in a clean, washed wineglass—the picture of refined taste. But we forget that the grapes have been pressed for their fragrant juice and the glass was blown after being put through scorching flames. And we, being human, are both the blood and the skin with a desperate need to be cleaned and filled.

I was tired of the daily fire and often would say to Nicole (referring to Yah), "Someone doesn't like me."

My mother's mental health continued to deteriorate, and her visits to the psych unit became more frequent. I was on a first-name basis with all three shifts of nurses, and I was so thankful to Kathy for her genuine love for my mother. It was a liability to keep someone as volatile as Mama in that quaint assisted-living home, but with some hypervigilance and a little finesse, Kathy managed to keep the peace along with everyone's well-being, until 2013 when the diagnosis was made. Mom's dementia had developed into fullblown Alzheimer's. The prognosis meant that she would eventually lose her cognitive abilities and finally ... her life.

Even if she forgot me, my love would *never* forget her.

NOTE

1. "America's Friendliest Towns," *Forbes*, accessed June 25, 2018, www.forbes.com /pictures/mhj45mdme/9-huntington-woods-mi/#4166659d3881.

20

THE GOOD SON

For even the Son of Man came not to be served but to serve others.

Mark 10:45

What must it be like to lose yourself? To stop knowing who you are. To forget your likes, dislikes, address, allergies, shoe size, favorite food, and the color of your own eyes. To misplace countless memories—decades on record—losing the combination to the vault and the treasure stored inside. To forget your wedding day, your spouse's name, your children, your grandchildren, the city you live in, the town of your birth, what planet you're on.

What do we look like without the past to color our present? Where do we go without a future? Can anyone see us? Does anyone want to?

I shared every step of my mother's journey with Sinclair via long-distance calls. He and I had dual power of attorney, but since I was

Mama's sole conservator, I made the day-to-day decisions regarding her health and personal care.

My brother hadn't seen Mama since my wedding more than fifteen years before. I never knew why he stayed away so long, nor did I ask. I was just happy to see him again. His visit was kept under wraps as a surprise. Holding a bouquet of flowers, Sinclair entered the room, and Mama instantly took him in her arms. She cried for several minutes, unable to stop.

Then, as quickly as the joy of her reunion appeared, it abruptly vanished. Like a pendulum swinging from elation to irritation, her mood changed, becoming agitated with the both of us. Poor Sinclair wasn't prepared for the sudden shift in her temperament, and we left soon after.

On the drive home, my older brother broke down—it was all too much to take. I'd never seen him cry before. My heart hurt for him. And with his gratitude for all I had been doing to care for Mama came guilt from realizing the load I had been carrying.

There was little he could do from Texas, so we made a deal: he would assist me in paying for Mom's medications and also pray for me as I tended to her. And his prayers, financial support, and lifelong influence on me were never more evident.

Sinclair's visits to see Mom once or twice a year—when he could take off work—kept his face fresh in her mind. He loved her, and to show it in his own way, he began to volunteer at a dementia and Alzheimer's clinic in Austin. She may have been out of his sight but was never far from his heart.

Despite the exceptional care and attention Mama was getting, two strokes almost ended her life. Still, she hung on—like her father before her—with a peculiar strength that exceeded common physical limits. Let's face it—she came from the "Wright" stock.

———— • ————

It seemed we were all being broken and mended on a daily basis.

My relationship with Nicole had already survived one close call when a joking voice mail left by a friend almost waylaid our marriage. And though we had made it through some pretty tumultuous times, we came to yet another fork in the road.

In June of 2015, my wife and I admitted we simply couldn't get along. The arguments were nonstop, and it wasn't the kind of environment or example we wanted to set for our children. Up until that point, we had made compromises that helped our rapport, but the disagreements continued. No infidelity, no gambling, no drugs—just too many wounds and negative talk over each other.

We had finally reached an impasse and decided to separate.

As Nicole walked away, I stood in our kitchen and prayed fervently. Within seconds, I felt the Holy Spirit say, "You and Nicole built this marriage on the sand of your individual desires, not the Rock, Christ. If you want to save your marriage, you must die to yourselves and surrender it to Yah for His glory."

As soon as I relayed this message to Nicole, we prayed together and agreed to give counseling another try.

I felt leery going in. Men often get verbally beaten down in counseling sessions, and I didn't relish the thought of it happening to me. The misleading mantra "Happy wife, happy life" seemed to work only if the man stayed quiet. But I knew firsthand what happens when men bottle up their emotions: the results are spousal abuse, self-medicating, and extramarital affairs, to name a few.

Nicole and I have had several counselors within our seventeen-year marriage, but we had never experienced counseling like Dr. Tim and Ellie Broe gave to us. They taught us how the brain regulates our emotions and processes thoughts. This information, combined with biblical principles, helped us understand our established life habits and expectations that turned us either away from or toward each other.

Within the journey, we learned communication skills using compassionate curiosity instead of defensive judgment. Guided through the gridlock, we identified relational barriers in new ways, thus freeing us from ourselves. Our marriage was becoming more like Yah intended, extending grace and compassion to each other and filling the holes left by our own marriage demolition.

We were on our way to recovery.

Over the next year, Nicole and I consistently went to counseling and became closer than we could have imagined. Our listening and communication improved dramatically as I proactively found a tone that was respectful and rooted in love. Nicole was smiling again!

Out of the ashes our marriage was resurrected.

———— • ————

A woman's heart is a fragile thing. When she loses a piece of it, half of it, or all of it, you can see it in her face. Her eyes dim, and the exuberance in her voice wilts.

It crushed my heart when my mother began to notice that those she loved stopped coming to visit her.

"Dementia isn't contagious," she would say.

This is when I realized that human love is conditional, which is why forgiveness is essential, leading to the freedom we all need and desire.

The TV was off when I entered my mother's hospital room after she was admitted to the psych unit once again for severe paranoia. She sat quietly, subdued and sad. I took a seat next to her.

"I don't want to be here," she said just above a whisper. "I'm tired of being depressed. I want to be free, to feel joy again. And I want others to feel joy when they're with me."

What could I say to that? There it was—a lucid moment where she made complete sense. I held her hand and, with the gentlest voice within me, said, "Mama, it's time you let go of your past."

Tears began to flow as the dam broke, sending a tsunami of pain cascading down her face. We talked about the lynching of her father, her abusive first marriage to Sinclair Sr., and the death of my brother Larry. Then the room fell silent for several minutes.

Unexpectedly, she cried, "Lord Jesus, come into my heart."

"Mom, you never asked Him before?" I asked. With my family's background in the church, it was hard to believe.

"Yes," she said, "but I don't think He did because I didn't really believe." Like many professing Christians, Mama knew church culture but not Christ.

She continued, "I believe with all my heart that Christ died for me and rose from the grave."

The words were like music to me—the loveliest song I had ever heard her sing.

She was finally able to forgive the men who murdered her dad, her first husband for abusing her, and the boys who killed her son. Her face was radiant and peaceful. Her eyes sparkled. For years I prayed for us to become closer, but her heart was shut away, unable to see. Now, in the midst of this demoralizing mental disease, she could set it free. She released it to me.

———— • ————

It's terrifying to switch places with a parent. One minute they're washing you and changing your diapers; fast-forward forty years, and you're washing and changing them. That's when you learn that sacrifice is not always doing what you want to do but doing what someone else needs to have done that you don't want to do.

There was a morning when Mama became so disoriented and combative, her caretakers called me to help get her up and ready for the day. As I was combing her hair, suddenly, out of the fog of confusion, my mother found her way to me.

"Thank you," she said with a sense of relief, knowing that she had chosen the right words.

"You're welcome, Mama."

"Thank you, Jason. You just don't find a son like you every day. And I appreciate it."

"I appreciate you too, Mom, for everything you've done for me."

Then, with eyes brimming with tears, she said, "I couldn't do enough ... I just couldn't do enough."

It was one of those moments, those subtle gifts, you sometimes don't realize are gifts until much later. But her words were like gold to me as they melted years of guilt.

"You stood by me all the time. You've been such a good son—a wonderful child all my life. All my life, Jason."

"Thank you so much, Mama," I gently answered. "I needed to hear it."

"You've been a good boy … I had no problems with you. No problems at all."

"I was just thinking about the times I wasn't as good, just being young," I said, as if I wasn't completely convinced that youth was enough to excuse the things I now wished I could take back.

"You *had* to be young. You had to be you! Nothing wrong with that. I knew you loved me, so it didn't matter. It was all right."

The love in the room was powerful. A love letter to remember her by. A gift.

———— • ————

Toward the end of my mother's life, the darkness descended like a curtain dowsing any light filtering in from the outside. Delusional, she cursed at me like a sworn enemy. Everything became a struggle. And when she took a fall that fractured her hip, Mom's condition made surgery impossible. Her frail, eighty-three-year-old state confined her to bed with a morphine drip, which slowed her heart rate and breathing.

It was like a nightmare she couldn't wake up from.

I phoned Sinclair, urging him to get a flight as soon as possible. He needed time with her while she was still able. He flew into Detroit and stayed with Mama for two weeks, keeping her in good spirits before returning home to resume work.

That Wright tenacity kept her going for nearly two more months with around-the-clock hospice care to manage her pain. But after four days of not eating or drinking, Mom was weak, bewildered, and losing the fight. When I walked into her room that day, I could see that her spirit was getting ready to leave.

The time had come to say good-bye.

Nicole brought Alexis and Jason Jr. to give Grandma a kiss as she prepared for her departure. My wife cried harder than I had ever witnessed before. She loved my mother like her own; Mama was family and a member not easily given up. To see my two favorite women together, united in love and now pulled apart in death—one staying with me, the other one leaving—was heart wrenching.

As Mama flew closer to the Son, she couldn't speak. But her eyes told a weary story of struggle and longing to break free of her confines of the flesh. I laid my head on her chest with tears saturating her nightgown, and with a mother's unfailing might, she wrapped her trembling arms around my head as I wept.

My heart then went to my brother Sinclair, aching for him to share this transitional moment with us. I dialed his number and he answered; then I placed the cell phone next to her face on speaker.

There are no words to truly describe the depth of that farewell. Two sons in tears, bidding their mama Godspeed as her change of address would place her at a distance only eternal love could reach. Mama cried her good-bye as she listened to Sinclair and me pour out our last bit of earthly affection on her like a salve to heal any hidden wounds we'd missed before it was too late. We told her how much we both loved her and appreciated what she had done and endured for us. That her sacrifices offered us a future that was brighter because of her.

After a time spent holding her, crying, and waiting, we were encouraged by Kathy to go home, understanding that as long as we didn't leave, Mama wouldn't leave.

Sleep was scarce that night as we anticipated the call. And as I lay there with my mind meandering through the backlog of life experiences with my mother, I recalled the priceless gift of a conversation we had months before.

"One of these days, Jason, I'm gonna have to go. And God will take care of you until you got to go. He will take care of you."

The words still echoed clearly, as if she were standing there next to my bed.

"One of these days, I'm going home with the Father. Jason, I want to see you."

"You'll see me," I assured her as I tenderly stroked her forehead.

"Jason, just be good; take care of yourself," she said as she cried through a heavy sigh. "I love you so much!"

"I love you too, Mama."

"You've been a good boy, the son of sons. God bless you, Jason."

That morning on April 29, 2016, at five o'clock, the world felt a little emptier when Mama went to be in the presence of the Most High. Her spirit had left, but what remained was a tiny wisp of a woman that—frail and petite—had overcome the world. Not a victim, not a casualty, but a resilient queen bound for eternal rest with the King of Kings.

For decades I thought power was based on how much weight you could lift and how many men you could knock out. Now I realize anyone untrained can lift a dumbbell or break a jaw. But real power is when a man can navigate through the pressures of this world without succumbing to his negative emotions.

To feel something painful and not push it away.

To cry, just cry.

Like a man.

EPILOGUE

*No life manifests more beauty than the one who is
broken! Stubbornness and self-love have given way to
beauty in the one who has been broken by God.*

Watchman Nee, *The Release of the Spirit*

As grateful as I was for having reconciled with my father before he died, before the six years I spent serving my mother, I was still living in pain. My festering father wound had infected my heart, even as I clung to hope for healing, knowing that Yah "is a rewarder of those who diligently seek Him" (Heb. 11:6 NKJV).

For decades I'd read countless books on fatherlessness and traveled to men's conferences, but it was in May 2015 when I found my treasure: The Crucible Project.

The crucible—a situation of severe trial leading to the creation of something new—was what moved me out of solitary confinement. This intensive Christian men's retreat gave me a safe space to be courageously transparent with counselors, to heal from trauma, and to discover my God-given masculinity.

From the time I was six years old until then, I had allowed Satan to haunt me with painful memories of my father, but I never allowed the Holy Spirit to bring to my remembrance the good that he did. Like many absent fathers, he didn't give fatherly affirmation and attention. He deeply loved me but did not know how to express it. As soon as I accepted this truth, my chest felt as if it was on fire as my heart purged the clots of resentment from my arteries.

I cried for hours, thanking Yah for my liberation. My father wound was finally healed.

My mother's transition immediately ushered in my own. The moment the Most High liberated Mama from her weary body, the door to my cell was unlocked—completely freeing me from emotional incarceration.

It was as if Yah said, "It is finished."

This freedom has healed my past, rejuvenated my marriage, fortified my family, and advanced my work through The Cave of Adullam Transformational Training Academy (CATTA).

My primary emphasis with CATTA recruits is on the importance of demonstrably ruling their emotions so they can unapologetically express them in a healthy way, without worry of condemnation from themselves or others. With the faithful help of my assistant instructor, Chris Norris, we work to instill the value of courageous transparency and spiritual strength, which is accomplished through our Emotional Stability Training (EST).

EST exposes the root of unresolved anger, anxieties, lack of focus, and fear while teaching our recruits how to introspectively confront and conquer their negative emotions with composure—a lesson they carry into adulthood.

While none of us are immune to a lack of confidence at times telling us we're never good enough, so many of our failures are due to a lack of mental fortitude needed to overcome the discouragement and weariness of battle. Just because we've broken through a challenge once—using brute force—doesn't mean we'll be able to do it again ... and *again*.

Consistent victory comes from a much deeper place.

The Most High said, "No one will succeed by strength alone" (1 Sam. 2:9). Men need to realize that "the fight" is won within themselves before it can be won out in the world. "As [a man] thinks in his heart, so is he" (Prov. 23:7 NKJV). In other words, what you *think* can directly influence what you experience and how you experience it.

A perfect example of this can be seen in a video of a CATTA recruit named Bruce that went viral with nearly a hundred million views worldwide. I think the struggle in that clip is one many men can identify with: self-doubt rooted in a fear of failure. Visit YouTube and check out "Breaking through Emotional Barriers" and see whether you don't agree.[1]

In the wake of that video's impact, our phones started ringing off the hook with everyone from doctors and pastors to military and police officers. What a blessing it was to see that a number of male soldiers and cops felt free enough to cry openly to our staff—people they'd never met. Several of these men admitted it was the first time they had cried since childhood. They saw something in that little boy they wanted for themselves—the freedom to feel vulnerable.

To date, our nonprofit The Yunion has reached over ten thousand Metro Detroit youth, with CATTA currently listing more than four hundred boys on its waiting list. This only confirms that there is a great need for the redefining of what "being a man" means and how it looks in contemporary society.

Regardless of ethnicity or economic status, we all face barriers, daily hardships that seem to keep us from moving forward in a healthy direction. But instead of letting those challenges beat you down, use them to develop the faith, focus, fortitude, and follow-through that can and will lift you up.

Perhaps you're feeling it's time to break the chain that was passed from father to son, to begin a new life with peace at its center. To breathe easy in the midst of the chaos and to act and respond in the strength that comes with knowing who you are and what you're made of. That includes compassion, gentleness, courage, and a fiery spirit. And at the core of you lives a power so great, nothing can dominate or destroy it—the power of love.

Adhere to these wise words: "He who is slow to anger is better than the mighty, and he who rules his spirit, than he who captures a city" (Prov. 16:32 NASB). An undeniable calm abides in that kind of depth. You don't need to prove yourself to anyone. You are designed to feel deeply. It's how you were made. You are hu*man*.

I know my story of generational abuse and abandonment is a familiar one, but as you can see, that's not how my story ends. That's not how *your* story has to end. As I take a moment and look back at my own journey, I can honestly say I've finally arrived at a place where I can thank the Most High for the tests and tribulations that have made me who I am today. If I hadn't prayed for Him to break me, I could not have accomplished all I have and all I still have to do.

That goes for you too, my brother.

If you're in "prison" reading this, I invite you to walk out of your cell right now. With Yah's help, you can. And when you do, something amazing will happen: you'll no longer be a victim of past trauma, shackled behind walls of negative emotions. But you'll be a free man who has conquered the worst and can now cry with the strongest.

I pray that healing overtakes you, that you will live freely from your authentic self, and that it propels you into a fuller, brighter future—a future filled with hope, love, joy, and *tears*.

NOTE

1. "Breaking through Emotional Barriers," July 26, 2016, YouTube video, 5:25, www.youtube.com/watch?v=ooAOc9Fwg0U.

I would love to hear my brother Larry play music, and sometimes I'd try to join him.

In my backyard at twelve years old trying my best to learn martial arts without a teacher.

Sixteen-year-old
Mystro on the flex!

The first love of my
life. Miss you Mama.

Here I'm pictured with my family after receiving the General Motors African Ancestry Network award for CATTA.

Teaching, training, and transforming boys, young men, and families in CATTA.

RECOMMENDED RESOURCES

Cry Like a Man

This is a comprehensive website for men to learn how to "cry," while being sharpened by other men in a safe space. Here you'll find inspirational and informational blogs and videos, emotional and mental health resources, forums, and support groups in your area. www.crylikeaman.com

The Crucible Weekend

Unlike any Christian men's retreat you've attended, The Crucible Weekend is designed to challenge you to take a hard look at what is and is not working in your life. Wrestle with God in a safe space and discover new truths about yourself and embrace your God-given masculinity. Man by man, this work is changing hearts, marriages, families, churches, careers, and cities. www.thecrucibleproject.org

The KING Movement

KING is a national Christian Men's Movement geared toward strengthening men in their personal relationship with Jesus Christ by providing brotherhood, encouragement, accountability, knowledge, and fellowship. The name KING is an acronym for Knowledge, Inspiration, and Nurture through God. KING is a nondenominational movement that seeks to unite true Bible-believing Christian men across racial, denominational, generational, and political lines. www.kingmovement.com

Thursday Prayer Call: 712-432-0075 | Code: 514320

BMe Community

BMe is the largest social entrepreneur fellowship in the US for black men. BMe, which stands for Black Male Engagement, is an award-winning network of community builders known for defining people by their positive contributions to society and enlisting incredible black men who inspire us to be better together. Headquartered in Miami, Florida, BMe also operates in Akron, Baltimore, Detroit, Louisville, Philadelphia, and Pittsburgh.

www.bmecommunity.org

Edge Venture

This incredible experiential retreat uses biblical principles and proven communal techniques to help men connect with the Holy Spirit and guide them into looking at the things that are preventing them from fully living liberated lives.

www.edgeventure.org

CBMA

The Campaign for Black Male Achievement (CBMA) is a national membership network that seeks to ensure the growth, sustainability, and impact of leaders and organizations committed to improving the life outcomes of black men and boys. CBMA is the only organization that both supports local leaders on the ground while at the same time amplifying and catalyzing the movement for black male achievement around the country.

www.blackmaleachievement.org

National Suicide Prevention Lifeline

Suicide is not inevitable for anyone. By starting the conversation, providing support, and directing help to those who need it, the National Suicide Prevention Lifeline can prevent suicides and save lives.

www.suicidepreventionlifeline.org

Phone: 800-273-8255

The Protectors

Unlike traditional anti-bullying efforts that focus primarily on reforming children who bully and which are historically ineffective,

The Protectors focuses primarily on the potential strength, heroic desire, and rescuing capacity of bystanders, transforming them into what is called "alongside standers." The Protectors also provide assertiveness training for targets, help authorities dispel the many damaging myths about bullying, and inspire children who bully to employ their power in life-affirming directions instead.
www.theprotectors.org

National Institute of Mental Health

Many mental illnesses affect both men and women; however, men may be less likely to talk about their feelings and seek help. Recognizing the signs that someone may have a mood or mental disorder is the first step toward getting treatment and living a better life. Find help in your area.
www.nimh.nih.gov
Phone: 866-615-6464

Inception

A dynamic new approach to mind and body fitness and wellness, Inception is designed specifically for today's hectic, stress-filled work styles and lifestyles. Inception's comprehensive approach to self-care relieves stress, releases trauma, and alleviates depression.
www.inceptionep.com
Phone: 248-436-2606

Books

- *No More Christian Nice Guy* by Paul Coughlin—why being nice instead of good hurts men, women, and children
- *The Father You've Always Wanted* by Ed Tandy McGlasson—how God heals your father wounds
- *The Release of the Spirit* by Watchman Nee—breaking our outward man so that the inward man may come out and be seen
- *Developing Positive Self Images and Discipline in Black Children* by Dr. Jawanza Kunjufu—examining the complete child and all the factors that potentially affect their future
- *Deadly Emotions* by Dr. Don Colbert—understand the mind-body-spirit connection that can heal or destroy you

Articles

- www.psychologytoday.com/us/blog/emotional-freedom/201007/the-health-benefits-tears.
  Crying is not only an emotional release but also has special health benefits.

- www.nytimes.com/1982/08/31/science/biological-role-of-emotional-tears-emerges-through-recent-studies.html.
  Crying is healthy.

ACKNOWLEDGMENTS

The Most High: Although I have so much to be grateful for, I'd rather spend this time praising You than thanking You. You are the sustainer of my soul, the source of my daily joy and peace. It's only in You that I live, move, and have my being. Your love is unrivaled, and Your mercy is unceasing. I stay in awe of who You are and amazed at what You do; no other gods come close to You. I praise You for ordering my steps and my stops. I praise You for gracefully orchestrating my tests and my trials. I praise You for prompting me to pray to be broken. Now I understand who I am here to please. For I know that with one sin, I could be abandoned by everyone and lose everything. But through Your Son Yahushua, I can repent unto You, and You will eagerly return unto me. Hallelu *Yah*!

Nicole: By far, the best decision I ever made was marrying you. I have truly obtained favor from the Most High. You sacrificed your body to give me a beautiful daughter and son—a family life I never experienced growing up. Thank you for loving me when I didn't love myself. Your optimistic outlook on life stills the symptoms of my traumatic past so I can enjoy the present. Thank you for supporting every vision Yah gave me, eagerly willing to help me bring them to fruition. Although I do not know what my future may hold, I'm blessed as long as I am holding you. I love you beyond what words could express.

Alexis: I fell in love with you when my eyes first saw your face. You literally changed my life. You have surpassed every expectation I could ever have for you; there is truly nothing else you could possibly do to make me prouder. You have always been my heart. I love you so much!

Jason: I couldn't have prayed for a better son. As a baby you were my pacifier, stilling my soul from the cares of this world. And today, as a boy, you make my heart proud. You may not know it, but you are my daily source of encouragement that keeps me striving to become a better man. I love you with all of my heart.

My mother: Mama, I don't know where to begin, but I will let my tears talk. I miss you so much. You have always been there for me. Your love stayed rooted in who I was and not what I did (good or bad). You were the closest I would ever get to experiencing unconditional love on earth. Now you're gone. My heart breaks as I cry and type this because I know I will never experience human love close to yours. Thank you for bestowing a love on me that my heart will never forget. I love you.

My father: Dad, thank you for making it right when it mattered the most. I love you.

Sinclair: I can say without reservation that without you being the light of Christ in my life, I would not be the radical man of the Most High I am today. Your decades of prayers, coupled with active love, guided me to light when I was lost in this dark world. Thank you, bro, for modeling faith instead of just preaching it. I love you.

Larry: I was so young when you were taken from us and did not realize how much my soul missed you until I wrote this memoir. We were alike in so many ways, I know we would have had a beautiful relationship. I love you, and I pray I will see you again.

Olivia: I can't tell you how many times your love and support kept me encouraged when I wanted to give up. I love you so much and am thankful we grow closer every year.

Uncle Clarence: Thank you for being the father figure I needed during my middle and high school years. You've made such an impact on my life that my eyes water whenever I talk about how Yah used you to teach me a work ethic. I deeply love you and Aunt Gladys.

My extended family: Dad and Mama Smith, Natalie, Tracey, Tawnya, Jon, and Bruce—thank you for being the close-knit family I've always longed for. I love you all so much.

Gabriel: It is written, "There is no greater love than to lay down one's life for one's friends" (John 15:13). Although we don't hang like we used to, we have a bond that can't be broken. We've both risked our lives for each other. There's no doubt you're my brother from another mother. I love you.

Vic: Thank you for making me laugh when my heart was heavy. Thank you for listening when I needed to vent. You've *always* been there. I love you.

My spiritual son, Chris: Thank you for your faithful service to the boys and young men in The Cave of Adullam. I couldn't do this without you. You are truly my Elisha, and I pray when it's my time to move on, Yah will give you a double portion of the Spirit He gave me. I love you.

My spiritual brother, Ron: Whenever I was in need, I could always count on you. Thank you for consistently being a source of encouragement in my life, especially when writing this memoir. You are truly like a brother to me, and I love you like one.

Our marriage counselors and friends, Dr. Tim Broe and Ellie: You two are simply amazing! Thank you for sacrificially pouring into Nicole and me. You both are a godsend. I love you.

To all my friends who supported me through the difficult process of writing this book: Thank you for your encouraging words and fervent prayers that kept me focused until it was completed. I love you all.

The Yunion staff and board of directors: Your support and dedication has been immeasurable. I thank the Most High daily for aligning me with co-laborers in Christ who I can sincerely call my friends.

To the pastors and mentors in my life: Thank you for guiding and praying for me and my family along the way. I love and thank you all.

Kimberly: We did it! Thank you for not only believing in me by seeking a deal for this book but also for helping me write my journey to freedom from emotional incarceration. You gracefully pushed me through the difficult process of revisiting my traumatic past. You are an awesome writer and coach. You truly deserve to be recognized with the best.

Alice: Thank you for believing in me. The thought of it still humbles me today. You have been rock steady throughout the writing process. I am so thankful for you. Your words of affirmation and prayers kept me encouraged, while your coaching kept me focused. You are so special, truly salt and light in this world. Thank you.

Wendi: Oh, what would I do without my fiery excellentist! Since the first day we met, I knew we were cut from the same cloth. Your desire for righteousness was refreshing to my soul and encouraged me. You are truly an amazing person and friend. Thank you!

Toben: My brother, thank you for boldly speaking from your heart during our first meeting. That moment not only garnered my respect for you but also saved this memoir. I look forward to growing our friendship.

JamieLyn: You are such a blessing. Thank you for checking up on me whenever you saw I was in need of prayer. Your passion for helping the disadvantaged inspires me to be more like Christ and boldly speak up for those who cannot speak for themselves. Your unwavering leadership with marketing this book kept me focused. Thank you.

My Cook Tribe: I will never forget the day I saw all of your faces during our first video conference call. I was humbled to tears to see so many believe in me. Thank you so much for undergirding God's vision for this memoir. It truly took a tribe to make this happen.